Biblical Wisdom:

Your Key to Success

J. Carl Laney

[signature: J. Carl Laney]

"Wisdom has the advantage of giving success."
Ecclesiastes 10:10

Copies available from CreateSpace.com,
Amazon,com and Amazon.co.uk
Copyright 2017 by J. Carl Laney
ISBN 13-978-1543297126
ISBN 10-1543297129
Printed in the United States of America

Biblical Wisdom

Table of Contents

To the glory of the One "in whom are hidden all the treasures of wisdom and knowledge"
(Colossians 2:3)

Biblical Wisdom

Introduction:
THE SEARCH FOR SUCCESS

Who hasn't longed for some lucky break—the right investment, that job promotion, that recognition which would spell *success?*

We all want to rise to the top, achieve our objectives, and report to our family, friends and associates, "Mission accomplished—successfully!" The question is, "What must a person know and do to live successfully?"

There are many theories of success. Some claim the secret is optimism, saying that we must "believe in ourselves." Others suggest that clothing is the key; we must "dress for success," wearing clothes befitting the position we seek. Still others argue for the survival of the fittest: to be successful, we must forget about others and put ourselves first.

Perhaps you too have joined in the search for success with the hope of economic prosperity, kindled by various amounts of faith, optimism and greed. Many people are pumping themselves up with "the power of positive thinking" or the blind hope that "something good is going to happen to me today." But do these attitudes really put us on the road to success?

Many people with their Madison Avenue wardrobes, shiny new cars, and latest electronic gadgets appear to have attained success. But if they could see a little further down the road of life, they would realize that in spite of the way things appear, in reality they are heading for disaster.

The Choice for Success
Success or failure in life depends a lot upon the choices we make. True, some failure is the result of circumstances over which we have little control. A classic example comes from naval history.

Escorting an arctic convoy in Murmansk in March 1942, the HMS *Trinidad* fired a torpedo at a passing German destroyer. The torpedo shot toward its target. Then, probably because the icy arctic water froze its steering mechanism, it slowly curved around in a semicircle until it headed straight toward the *Trinidad*. The torpedo scored a direct hit, and put the ship out of commission.

Certainly, some failures are the result of unavoidable circumstances. But many—perhaps most—are the natural consequences of wrong choices. Many of us choose misfortune because we have not discovered the key to success. Even hard working and well deserving people fail sometimes because they seek success the world's way, according to the world's standard. They have yet to discover the key to success that is tucked away in the Bible, God's Word.

Without God's key to success, we tend to make choices that result in foul-ups—financial bondage, unfulfilled marriages, and frustration in daily living. Wrong choices bring confusion and disorder to our personal lives, family relationships, and career pursuits. Our emotional well-being becomes impaired. We are weighed down by disappointment, failure, and guilt. Life loses its sparkle.

Most of us are aware of the consequences of wrong choices and unwise decisions. We've all been down that road before. But things can be different—if we know God's key to success.

No doubt, you would like to know what makes the difference between success and failure. You would love to be successful—a successful student, successful as a wife and mother, successful as a husband and father, successful in your career. Like most people today, you rightly desire to be the best person you can be in light of your God-given gifts and abilities. But what must you know and do to live successfully?

Introducing the Sages
The religious community of ancient Israel recognized three main sources of divine instruction (Jeremiah 18:18). The

people looked to the priests for instruction from the law (Torah), to the prophets for contemporary application of God's truth, and to the wise for counsel and guidance in daily living; wisdom pounded out in the crucible of experience by generations of sages.

The principles taught by these wise men and women provided answers to the questions of God's struggling people. As these principles passed the test of time and experience, they were written down and clustered together into books. God inspired the recording of these guidelines and principles, and they are preserved for us as the Wisdom Literature of the Hebrew Bible. We know them today as the books of Job, Psalms, Proverbs, Ecclesiastes, and the Song of Solomon. The teachings of these ancient books contain God's key to success.

The value of this ancient Wisdom Literature is not fully appreciated today, due in part to the puzzling statements and riddles found in these books. Some of these perplexing statements are intentional, planned by the sages to cause us to ponder and meditate on their ideas. However, the rewards of studying the Wisdom Books far surpass the effort applied in understanding their message.

No portion of the Bible has had a more dramatic effect on my personal life than the Wisdom Books. They have given me a new and deeper appreciation of life—its joys, its struggles, its complexities. In these books I have found God's key for success!

Questions of Life

The wisdom of ancient Israel is as fresh and applicable today as it was when it was first written. Among the questions and issues that the Wisdom Books address are the following:

1. Why does God allow good people to suffer? How should we respond to seemingly unjust suffering?
2. How should God's people deal with life's frustrations? Should they maintain an attitude of grim determination to survive, or is there a better way to cope with frustration?

3. What is God's attitude regarding sex? It is sex merely for the purpose of procreation, or was it designed for exquisite pleasure?
4. What are the benefits of sexual purity? What are the dangers of unrestrained sexual indulgence?
5. How should God's people view their careers? Is work something to delight in or endure? What should be our attitude toward work?
6. What principles of stewardship should guide our spending, investing and giving? How can financial independence be achieved?
7. What place should worship have in the lives of God's people? Must worship always be straitlaced, solemn and boring? How can we worship "in spirit and truth"?
8. How can we build a satisfying and lasting marriage? How important is the physical side of marriage?
9. How do we find meaning and fulfillment in our homes and family life? How should we discipline our children?
10. What are the characteristics of the successful man and woman?

This book is written for people like you—people who desire to live a balanced and successful life—enjoying life while enduring trials; maintaining sexual purity, yet enjoying the blessing of the physical aspect of marriage; working hard without neglecting family life and the place of rest and recreation.

The Search for God's Answers
Our search for a balanced and successful life will take us back into the Hebrew Bible to hear the voices of the sages, the wise teachers, the counselors of ancient Israel. We will ask questions and strive for personal application as we discover the answers. Some of the issues we will consider are too complex to be fully resolved this side of eternity.

But we will identify these issues and avoid the frustration of looking for answers that God has not yet given us.

The key to success for which so many in the twenty-first century are searching is available to us. If we are willing to seek, we shall find.

We are about to embark on a life-changing adventure! We cannot interact with the wise counsel of Israel's divinely inspired sages and go on living as we did in the past. As a result of our study together, we will develop a biblical philosophy of life—a life balanced by the wise lessons from the Wisdom writers. We will learn to measure success by God's standard and pursue success God's way. Success or failure—the choice is up to us.

"Life is a play for which we have no change to rehearse," says Jaques, the incurable cynic in Shakespeare's, *As You Like It*. There is a great deal of truth to these words. We make our entrance onto the stage of this life, play our respective roles, and receive either applause for success or disapproval for failure. To make fools of ourselves in life's unrehearsed drama would be tragic.

We have only once chance to make good, so as we are thrust out on the stage of life, we should seek guidance to help us perform well. The Wisdom literature of the ancient Hebrew scriptures serves as a handbook on life to help us get through our part successfully. It is a partial script, a handbook on the art of living successfully.

We must study the handbook well. With the insights offered on these pages, the wisdom of ancient Israel will enable us to better enjoy life and live more successfully. May we then receive God's appraisal, "Well done, My good and faithful servant. You sought wisdom, followed its principles, and lived your life successfully."

Chapter 1
GOD'S KEY TO SUCCESS

Little things can sometimes mean the difference between success and failure. Take, for example, the fate of the tanker, *Mobiloil.*

Two minutes after midnight, on March 19, 1984, the super-tanker Mobiloil ran aground on a rocky reef in the Columbia River. The ship smashed into the reef so hard that gashes 150 feet long were torn in the 1½ inch-thick steel hull, spilling more than a thousand barrels of heavy industrial oil into the river. The damage was so severe the tanker had to be scrapped.

Investigation into the cause of the accident revealed that the rudder of the tanker had jammed because of a missing cotter pin the size of a large bobby pin. The ship was lost for the lack of a sixteen-cent part that apparently was not put back in place after a recent overhaul. The three-inch pin was the key to the proper functioning of the ship's rudder. Without it, the vessel was on the course of inevitable disaster.

Success in life often depends on the little things we need to know and do. We are often tempted to ignore them because they appear so simple and obvious, such as the one hidden away in the much neglected Book of Ecclesiastes. Here we discover that "Wisdom has the advantage of giving success" (10:10). *The Jerusalem Bible* translation captures the emphasis of the verse: "The reward given by wisdom is success."

It sounds so simple, yet this is one of the most significant and profound statements in all of Scripture. Without a firm grasp of this truth, we are no better off than the *Mobiloil*, cruising through life with a missing cotter pin.

Success in life is the natural result of applying God's wisdom to the circumstances and situations we encounter. The wisdom found in God's Word serves as a guide for living successfully according to God's plan. Generally speaking, the successful person is the wise person—the one who is able to take insights into God's ways and apply them to daily life.

A Definition of Wisdom

What is wisdom? How is it different from knowledge? The Hebrew word translated "wisdom" *(hokmah)* is used to describe the skill needed to make the ceremonial clothing for Israel's high priest and the craftsmanship required to do fine metal work (Exodus 28:3; 31:3,6). It is also used of the tactics employed in a successful military campaign (Isaiah 10:13). Skill and ability are basic to the biblical concept of wisdom.

But does mere skill and ability make one wise? Someone might be clever or shrewd, but God's wisdom involves more than this. The wisdom of the Bible is founded on faith in a personal God who is holy and just, who expects certain things of His people. The wisdom of the Bible reflects a recognition of and conformity to the righteous will of God. The wise person is one who acknowledges God's direction and pursues what He has revealed as the best way to live.

Hebrew wisdom is the voice of reflection and experience. But it is more. Biblical wisdom is based on observable laws of nature and divinely revealed guidelines for the ethical, social, political, and economic affairs of life. From a scriptural viewpoint, wisdom is founded on revealed principles of right and wrong. Wisdom isn't just book learning. It is practical rather than merely theoretical knowledge.

Wisdom is the practical application of knowledge. Charles Haddon Spurgeon, London's great Baptist preacher, expanded this definition:

> Wisdom is the right use of knowledge. To know is not to be wise. Many men know a great deal, and are all the greater fools for it. There is no fool so great a fool as a

knowing fool. But to know how to use knowledge is to have wisdom.[1]

Wisdom is the application of our knowledge of God's way of doing things. Wisdom is the art of being successful through the application of God's truth to life's experiences.

The Example of Solomon

Since wisdom is God's key to success, it is only logical that we would desire to be wise. Most of us would settle for being the wisest person in our family or community group. Israel's King Solomon attained a worldwide reputation for great wisdom. So extraordinary was he that "all the earth was seeking the presence of Solomon, to hear his wisdom which God had put in his heart" (1 Kings 10:24).

Solomon's wisdom is highlighted in the familiar account of his dealing with the two harlots (1 Kings 32:16-28). One of two infants had died. Now both women claimed to be the mother of the living child. One of the harlots accused the other of exchanging the dead baby for her living one. The other woman insisted that the living child was hers. How as Solomon to decide?

After hearing the arguments, the king said, "Get me a sword." He then ordered a servant to divide the living child in two, giving "half to one and half to the other." Of course, Solomon had no intention of killing the living child, knowing that the maternal instinct to save the child's life would enable him to identify the true mother. Faced with the alternatives, the true mother responded, "Oh, my lord, give her the living child, and by no means kill him." The other woman insisted that the child be divided.

Solomon pronounced his decision. "Give the first woman the living child, and by no means kill him. She is his mother." This remarkable ruling enhanced Solomon's reputation throughout the land. The Israelite people recognized that God had truly given Solomon wisdom to administer justice.

---

[1] Tyron Edwards, ed. *The New Dictionary of Thoughts* (Standard Book Company, 1961), p. 729.

How did Solomon happen to acquire such wisdom? The answer is found in 1 Kings 3:5-14. While worshiping at Gibeon, the Lord appeared to Solomon in a dream and offered to give him whatever he wanted.

While he could have chosen virtually anything—a magnificent vineyard in Galilee, a gold-plated chariot, or a villa on Mount Carmel—Solomon chose something that would ultimately benefit others. He asked for wisdom. "So give your servant an understanding heart to judge your people to discern between good and evil" (1 Kings 3:9).

God answered Solomon's prayer and gave him wisdom and discernment which surpassed that of the wise men of the East and the sages of Egypt. During his lifetime Solomon authored 3,000 proverbs and composed 1,005 songs (1 Kings 4:32). His wisdom is recorded for us in Psalm 72 and 127, Proverbs, Ecclesiastes, and the Song of Solomon.

Is God's wisdom available only for the elite few, such as Solomon, or can others share it too? What is the source of wisdom? How may it be acquired? Let's consider what the wisdom writers have to say about wisdom and learn more about God's key to success.

The Source of Wisdom

If we were to ask Solomon, "Where should we begin our search for wisdom?" he would most certainly direct us to God Himself, who was his great source of wisdom. In Proverbs 2:6 Solomon declared, "For the LORD gives wisdom; from His mouth come knowledge and understanding." Daniel similarly acknowledged, "Let the name of God be blessed forever and ever, for wisdom and power belong to Him.... He gives wisdom to wise men" (Daniel 2:20-21). The writer of James agreed: "If any of you lacks wisdom, let him ask of God, who gives to all people generously and without reproach, and it will be given to him" (James 1:5).

I once assumed that wisdom could be found in a book or acquired with age and experience. But books often present confusing and contradictory theories. And many of us fail to learn the lessons of experience. Elihu, Job's young friend, was convinced that wisdom does not always accompany old age. He said, "The abundant in years may not be wise, nor may elders understand justice" (Job 32:9).

It is encouraging to know that wisdom is not exclusively for either the elderly or the educated. God's wisdom is within the grasp of us all. But wisdom will not arrive at our doorstep uninvited. While it is within the grasp of all, wisdom comes only to those who diligently seek it. There is one requirement for attaining wisdom. We must desire it so much that we are willing to yield our own ideas in favor of God's truth.

In Proverbs 8 wisdom is personified as a woman. Lady Wisdom is set in stark contrast with Madam Folly, and is portrayed as giving an invitation to all who will receive her. "I love those who love me; and those who diligently seek me will find me" (8:17). Lady Wisdom offers success and fullness of life to those who respond to her invitation.

Solomon declared that wisdom is available to those who will "seek her as silver, and search for her as for hidden treasures" (Proverbs 2:4). Later he added, "The beginning of wisdom is: Acquire wisdom; and with all your acquiring, get understanding" (Proverbs 4:7).

What it takes to acquire wisdom is not brains or opportunity, but decision. It is ours if we want it and will strive to attain it. God will give us wisdom if we are willing to diligently seek it. But where shall we begin our search? What is the first step to success?

The beginning of wisdom

The mastery of any skill is dependent upon learning the fundamentals. A successful football coach spends a great deal of time with his players reviewing the fundamentals of the game – blocking, tackling, and receiving the ball. In our pursuit of success, we must first master the fundamentals.

The fundamental lesson in our study of successful living is the concept of the "fear of the Lord." Solomon declared, "The fear of the Lord is the beginning of wisdom, and knowledge of the Holy One is understanding" (Proverbs

15

9:10). The fear of the Lord is the first and most important step in our pursuit of wisdom. The fear of the Lord is the theme of Proverbs (1:7) and the conclusion of Ecclesiastes (12:23). The "fear of the Lord" characterizes both the ideal woman (Proverbs 31:30) and the successful man (Psalm 147:11; Proverbs 22:4; Ecclesiastes 8:22). The fear of the Lord is the most important part of our search for success. Without it, we are bound to fail.

The fear of God – is it like the dread we sense during the hour before surgery? Is it the trembling we feel after narrowly avoiding a rear end collision? Are Christians expected to tremble before their awesome, holy God?

There is a place for real fear in relationship to God's eternal judgment of unbelievers or His discipline of disobedient Christians. The "fear of the Lord," however, is not the same as being afraid. Psalm 112:1 reads "how blessed is the man who fears the Lord, who greatly delights in his commandments." The word *blessed* can be translated "happy." Happiness and fear are mutually exclusive.

Fearing God is equated in Proverbs 2:5 with knowing God. If we truly know God and appreciate His attributes, we can't help but having a healthy respect for His person. If we know that God is holy, just, sovereign, loving, and all powerful, we can't help but respect and want to please Him.

As a professor at Western seminary, I am accountable to the academic Dean. I have an appreciation for his office and respect for his person. I don't tremble when I pass him in the hall or when I sit with him in the faculty lunch room. Yet, I do recognize that he holds me accountable for the quality of my classroom instruction. I want to know and meet his standards.

In the same way, fearing the Lord means knowing Him—knowing His character, His standards, His demands. It means responding to God in light of our knowledge of who He is and what he wants for us as His people.

The wisdom writers show us how this fear is applied to life. The parallel structure of Job 28:28 associates the "fear of the Lord" with the words, "to depart from evil." A person demonstrates his "fear of the Lord" by departing from evil. In Psalm 111:10, "wisdom" is set in a parallel relationship with the words, "those who do His commandments." Again, we express our "fear of the Lord" by doing God's commandments.

The one who truly fears God does not stand around with trembling hands and knocking knees; he or she seeks to obey God and strives to do His will. As Ron Allen wrote, "The fear of Yahweh is not a terror before him, but a positive response to his majesty and glory, a readiness to worship and serve him, a recognition of who he is and who man is before him."[2]

Is it possible to fear God and also love Him? While fear and love seem to be opposite responses, it is clear from the Bible that God expects His people to do both. This is evident from the words of Moses: "And now, Israel, what does the Lord require from you, but to fear the Lord our God, to walk in all His ways and love Him, and to serve the Lord your God with all your heart and with all your soul, and to keep the Lord's commandments and His statutes which I am commanding you today for your good?" (Deuteronomy 10:12-13). Fearing God and loving God are not mutually exclusive concepts. As a child has respect for his parents whom he loves, so God's people must both love and fear Him.

The Benefits of Wisdom

Wisdom pays high dividends. The first and most notable dividend is success in life: "The reward given by wisdom is success" (Ecclesiastes 10:10).

Success does not mean becoming a millionaire, being a straight-A student, winning an Olympic gold medal, or being listed in the Guinness Book of World Records. We must be careful not to fall into the trap of viewing success from the world's viewpoint. The success wisdom promises

---

[2] Ronald B. Allen, *The Majesty of Man* (Portland, Oregon: Multnomah Press, 1984), 158.

does not necessarily mean having lots of money in the bank, becoming a corporate president, or owning a condo in the Bahamas.

Being successful does not mean that we won't have any problems. It *does* mean that we know how to apply God's wisdom in dealing with the various difficulties in life that we all encounter. Being successful means that by following God's guidelines we can avoid unnecessary misfortune, such as the devastating effects of sin in our lives; the shame and reproach that comes from violating God's standards of morality; the burden of financial entanglements; the stress and sorrow of marital failure; the depression that comes from groping for answers to unanswerable questions; the frustrations that come from an improper attitude regarding work; and the attitude of discontent about circumstances over which we have no control.

In addition to giving success, Scripture reveals that wisdom yields some other significant dividends:

1. Wisdom preserves the lives of its possessors (Ecclesiastes 7:12, Proverbs 14:27). All other things being equal, a wise person will live longer than a fool.
2. Wisdom makes us happier (Proverbs 3:18). This doesn't mean that we won't have problems, but wisdom will make us better able to cope with life's inevitable difficulties.
3. Wisdom results in our physical needs being met (Psalm 34:9-14). And what needs God does not meet, He will give us the grace to go without.
4. Wisdom yields honor (Proverbs 4:8; 22:4). The wise person will be recognized and sought out for counsel and instruction.
5. Wisdom leads to financial independence (Proverbs 6:1-5; 22:4). Wise people will be good stewards of their resources and avoid financial entanglements.

Your Choice

In his insightful commentary on Proverbs, the respected Jewish scholar, Dr. Abraham Cohen, highlighted the benefits of wisdom as he summarized the basic thesis of Israel's sages:

> They urge the fundamental thesis that the morally defective and willfully perverted stand in their own light, deny themselves the real joys of living, bring avoidable troubles upon their head and, though they may at times have a momentary triumph, ultimately fail. On the other hand, to conduct oneself in the light of wisdom means to get the best out of life, discover sources of strength which assure final victory over calamity and evil, and become a blessing to oneself and society.[3]

As with the *Mobiloil* tanker, small things often make a big difference—the difference between success and failure. Wisdom is one of those seemingly insignificant matters. Yet it is God's key to success in life.

Wisdom means that we can choose prosperity over adversity. We can choose the smooth path over the rocky road. We can choose success over failure. The "cotter pin" of success is *wisdom*. Only a fool would sail the unknown seas of life without it. But fools abound and the wise are few. Which will it be for you?

Study and Review Questions
1. Write your own definition of wisdom. What is the relationship between wisdom and success in life?
2. Solomon was the wisest man who ever lived. How did he gain his wisdom? How was his wisdom evidenced in Israel?
3. Where should you look for wisdom? Provide some scriptural support for your answer.

---

[3] A. Cohen, *Proverbs* in Soncino Book s of the Bible (London: The Soncino Press, 1946), xiii-xiv.

4. What does it mean to "fear the Lord"? How is this concept to be applied practically in our lives?
5. What is the relationship between the attitudes of love and fear in your walk with God? Is it possible for you to have both? Use an illustration to explain this.
6. Are there benefits of being wise? Of the benefits that accompanies wisdom, which of them are especially important to you?

Chapter 2
WHEN BAD THINGS HAPPEN

According to Solomon, being "successful" doesn't mean that we won't have to face trials or difficulties in life. In Ecclesiastes he wrote, "In the day of prosperity be happy, but in the day of adversity consider—God has made the one as well as the other" (7:14).

We live in a fallen world where the effects of sin, as a cancer, eat away at our lives. Things are not as they would have been had not Adam and Eve transgressed in the Garden. With their sin came sorrow, sickness, and death.

All people experience trials in life—even those who honor and serve God. As important as wisdom is in the pursuit of successful living, even great wisdom will not protect us from many of the difficulties and trials of life.

Del and Ellen Meliza were top caliber seminary students whom God led to serve as missionaries in Brazil. Their trial is reported in a letter sent shortly after the birth of their son:

> For those who have been praying for us and awaiting the news of the arrival of our second child, we are happy to announce the birth of David Earl on June 26th. He weighed 8 lbs., 10 ounces., and was 20 inches long.

But there was more that Del and Ellen had to say. Their letter continued:

> David Earl is an extra special gift from God for he is a Down's syndrome child. Because of this he will always remain mentally immature and physically handicapped.

Even successful servants of the Lord, like Del and Ellen, are not immune to trial. Bad things do happen to God's good people.

This fact of life was brought to my mind again when I read a letter from Sharon Wolfe, the wife of my former student, Ralph. Serving as missionaries in Kenya, Ralph and Sharon had gone to Mombasa, a coastal area of Kenya, for the weekend. There they enjoyed a beautiful time on the silky white beaches with coconut palms, coral

21

reefs, and aqua waves. Ralph had grown up in Kenya and was delighted to share this part of his childhood with Sharon and their daughter Anya.

> Traveling back along the Mombasa road, Ralph was driving a friend's VW bug. They were singing together. Ralph was squeezing Sharon's hand. The next thing Sharon remembers was the police pulling her out of the car.

The VW had run into a large truck that had stopped in the middle of the road with no lights or reflectors. Anya miraculously escaped injury. But Ralph was killed instantly. From her bed in Nairobi Hospital, Sharon wrote, "Yes, it seems like such a meaningless way to die—we all hope for death with more meaning."

Why does God allow good and godly people to suffer? Why do bad things happen to God's people? Is there wisdom from God's Word to help us live through the painful experiences and trials that will come our way?

Perhaps you have all raised similar questions over the sorrows or tragedies in your life. It may have been the death of a loved one, the breakup of a relationship, or the loss of a job. In such situations, we cannot help wondering why a righteous and good God would allow His people to go through such suffering.

How should we respond to physical and emotional affliction when it comes our way? It is possible to "suffer successfully"?

The Book of Job presents a classic study of the problem of suffering. Here we read of the tragedy and suffering that came into the life of a good and righteous man. We also see how he eventually triumphed over his tragedy. We can gain insight into the problem of suffering from the sage who tells Job's story.

Job's Tragedy (Job 1-2)

The first verse of the book introduces Job. "There was a man in the land of Uz, whose name was Job, and that man was blameless, upright, fearing God, and turning away from evil." He was not said to have attained sinless perfection, but Job is presented as a righteous man. Even the Lord testifies (twice!) to Job's unique moral and spiritual character (1:8, 2:3).

To understand Job's experience, we must recognize that his suffering was not due to sin in his life. Even in his calamity, Job did not sin (1:22) nor did he curse God, as Satan had predicted (1:11; 2:5).

As the story begins, the curtains of heaven are drawn back to reveal a drama of which Job was completely unaware. Among the angels of heaven appeared a visitor—our Adversary the devil—Satan himself. Like a proud parent, the Lord called Satan's attention to Job—a man of exemplary righteousness and godliness. But Satan seemed unimpressed. He explained that Job's good conduct was due to the protection and provisions of God. Satan reasoned, "Job is good because God is good to him."

Then Satan challenged, "But put forth Your hand now and touch all that he has; he will surely curse You to Your face" (1:11). In order to prove the genuineness of Job's character against Satan's challenge, God gave Satan permission to destroy all Job's possessions, including the lives of his children. This personal calamity was divinely designed to prove to Satan that Job's faith was genuine.

It is important to notice that Satan didn't have a "free hand" in his attack on Job. God clearly set limits on what Satan could do. God told Satan, "Behold, all that he has is in your power, only do not put forth your hand on him" (Job 1:12). Later, God spoke to Satan again, "Behold, he is in your power, only spare his life" (2:6). Job's suffering was not the result of God losing control of the situation. God permitted Job's suffering, but prescribed limits on what Job would endure. God remained sovereign over Job's experience.

The First Assault (1:13-22). Job was prospering and enjoying life when four staggering blows filled his world with sorrow. First, desert looters (*Sabeans*) attacked and killed Job's workers, stealing his oxen and donkeys.

Second, fire from heaven--perhaps lightning--killed his sheep and servants. Third, three bands of Chaldean raiders captured his camels, killing more of his servants. Fourth, a great wind blew down his son's house, killing all Job's children.

Yet, while Job lost all his children and property, he did not lose his faith. Job responded to this personal tragedy by worshiping God. Instead of cursing God, as Satan had predicted, Job blessed God. "The LORD gave and the LORD has taken away. Blessed be the name of the LORD" (1:21).

Job had no idea of the cosmic conflict that was at the background of his tragic experience. He didn't know why he was suffering. Yet his response to the tragedies proved wrong Satan's theory that Job was good merely because God was good to him.

The Second Assault (2:1-10). Satan is not one to give up easily. When God called attention to Job's steadfast character in spite of his personal loss, Satan argued that Job had accepted these losses in order not to endanger his own life and health. With the genuineness of Job's piety still in question, God gave Satan a second chance to test Job.

Satan's second assault took the form of physical suffering. Job was stricken with boils "from the sole of his foot to the crown of his head" (2:7). Medical opinion differs in its diagnosis of Job's disease. The symptoms included eruptions on the skin accompanied by intense itching (2:7-8), maggots in open flesh wounds (7:5), feverish nightmares (7:14), bad breath (19:17), pain in the bones (30:17, 30), and blackening of the skin (30:30).

Whatever job had, it wasn't pleasant. As was the custom of a mourner, he sat in a pile of ashes. Seeking relief from his affliction, Job scraped his itching sores with a piece of broken pottery.

Added to Job's suffering was the lack of support and encouragement by his wife. Distraught by the loss of her ten children, she suggested that Job renounce his faith:

"Curse God and die!" This is exactly what Satan had hoped Job would do. But Job responded, "Shall we indeed accept good from God and not accept adversity?" Job did not know why he was suffering, but he would not curse God. He maintained his faith while enduring his trial and did not sin.

Job's Struggle (Job 3-41)

Hearing of the tragic turn of events in Job's life, three of his friends came to Job "to sympathize with him and comfort him" (2:11). They had heard about Job's calamities, but were unprepared for what they found. Job's affliction had so distorted his physical appearance that his friends didn't even recognize him.

Job's friends appeared to be genuinely concerned for him and wanted to help him understand his suffering. But they didn't know what we know from reading chapters 1 and 2. Job's friends were convinced that suffering is always punishment for sin. Since their friend was suffering so severely, they concluded that Job must have been a great sinner.

Throughout this section of the book (chapters 3-41), Job interacted with his friends over their explanation for his suffering. Job continued to assert his innocence, insisting that his suffering couldn't be attributed to secret sin in his life. Job's friends continued to probe Job's conscience, trying to get him to admit his fault. They used some of the arguments others have used to explain our suffering.

Eliphaz the Mystic. Eliphaz, the first of Job's friends to speak, was a dreamer of dreams. He based his view regarding Job's suffering on personal experience and a mystical vision.

According to what Eliphaz had seen and experienced, the innocent and upright are spared calamity. On the other hand, "those who plow iniquity and those sow trouble harvest it" (4:8). Eliphaz argued that suffering was the immediate consequence of sin.

This thesis was confirmed by his hair-raising night vision. In a dream, Eliphaz heard a voice, "Can mankind be just before God? Can a man be pure before his Maker?" (4:17). The obvious answer to these rhetorical questions is "No" (cf. Romans 3:10-18). Applying his thesis to Job's situation, Eliphaz concluded that Job was suffering severely because he was guilty of great sin. He counseled Job to repent and accept God's discipline.

Bildad the Traditionalist. Bildad argued his views on the basis of tradition and consensus of opinion (8:8-10). He claimed to be in touch with what past generations had searched out. Bildad was quite impressed with the traditional viewpoints, believing that they offered the explanation for Job's suffering.

Bildad was confident that God would not pervert justice (8:3). Therefore, God would not permit Job to suffer without deserving it. He suggested that if Job were innocent, then God would intervene and restore Job's health and prosperity. Like Eliphaz, he counseled Job to seek God and be restored (8:5-6).

Zophar the Rationalist. Zophar, the third of Job's friends to speak, was a coldhearted rationalist. He appealed to a common-sense application of biblical doctrine. Since God knows all things, iniquity hidden in the human heart cannot escape His notice (11:11). He concluded that exceptional suffering is clear proof of exceptional guilt.

In keeping with his "common sense" way of understanding things, Zophar counseled Job to repent and be restored (11:13-17).

The Arguments Reconsidered. What of the arguments set forth by Job's friends? Are there faults in their logic?

Eliphaz argued from *experience*. The problem is that his experience was limited. Experience is a great teacher, but is lessons may not apply in every situation. Job's situation was certainly an exception to the norm, and the limited experience of Eliphaz didn't allow for any exceptions.

Bildad argued from *tradition*. Certainly there is nothing wrong with traditional viewpoints, as long as they are biblical. The problem comes when we elevate tradition above the authority of Scripture. Bildad was so locked into a traditional approach to suffering that he could not make an allowance in his system for Job's exception.

Zophar argued on the basis of a matter-of-fact *rationalism*. He was a clear-minded thinking with a solid theology. However, he allowed his rational approach to oversimplify the complex issues with which Job was struggling. There was not a breath of compassion or evidence of genuine, personal concern in his words. His chiding attitude shows how little he sensed Job's hurt or listened to his words.

Elihu the Young Man. The three friends probed Job's conscience and exhorted him to repent. Next the voice of a young man was heard. Elihu was angry at Job for justifying himself before God (32:2), and angry at Job's friends because they persistently condemned him, yet had no answer for Job's dilemma (32:3,12).

Unlike Job's friends, Elihu did not relate all suffering to sin. While he recognized that God may use suffering for disciplinary purposes (33:17), Elihu pointed out that suffering may be designed to teach us something (33:16; 36:10,22).

It is refreshing to hear from someone who does not condemn Job of sin. He did not ultimately answer Job's question as to why he was suffering, but he did direct Job's attention to the greatness of God, whose ways are beyond man's comprehension and scrutiny (33:1-20). Elihu's view on the cause of suffering was not as narrow and limited as Job's friends. He turned Job in the right direction.

God the Creator. The last one to address Job with regard to his suffering was God Himself. Human insight into Job's tragedy was exhausted. Now, God speaks.

God the Creator rebuked Job for his ignorance regarding the divine ordering of nature and life's events

(38:2-40:2). Yet never did the Lord condemn Job of sin. By not pronouncing him guilty, the theory of Job's three friends is laid to rest.

It may surprise us that the Lord offered no explanation for Job's suffering. In fact, He didn't even mention the problem. Instead, the Lord directed Job to His own greatness and power as Creator. In chapters 38-41, God showed Job that He controls the intricate details of all creation, which Job can only dimly understand. So Job must trust God to order the details of his life even though he does not fully understand God's doings.

God does not answer the theological question, "Why do the righteous suffer?" But He met the need of Job's heart by giving him a new revelation of Himself. Job's question as to why he was suffering evaporated in view of his new appreciation of God's greatness. God has not seen fit to give us the reason for everything He does. But the Book of Job sets forth a God so great that no answer is needed.

Job's Triumph (42)

In the conclusion, Job told God, "I have heard of You by the hearing of the ear; but now my eye sees You" (42:5). Job had a good deal of head knowledge about God prior to his personal calamities. But through his struggle, he gained new insight into God's character and attributes. He acquired a deeper understanding of God's sovereignty over creation and His providential care of His own.

Job was finally satisfied and able to deal successfully with his suffering not because of any answer he had received but because he had *met God!* Job experienced God in a new way, which enabled him to cope with the unanswered questions in his life. In the end, God restored Job to prosperity and prominence beyond that of his earlier years (42:10-17).

Responding to Suffering

Job's triumph leaves us with a note of hope, but not a mechanical answer to the problem of suffering. The complexity of the matter does not lend itself to being easily simplified. There are a number of possible explanations for our suffering:

1. Suffering may be divine punishment for sin, as in the cases of Achan (Joshua 7:20-26) and Ananias and Sapphira (Acts 5:1-11).
2. Suffering may be disciplinary or corrective, as with the Corinthians who were abusing the Lord's Supper (1 Corinthians 11:30-32).
3. Suffering may be the result of persecution, reflecting the world's hatred of Jesus and His followers (John 15:20; 16:33; 2 Timothy 3:12).
4. Suffering may be intended by God to prevent spiritual problems, as in the case of Paul's "thorn in the flesh" (2 Corinthians 12:7).
5. As in the case of the man born blind (John 9), suffering may be intended as an opportunity to display "the works of God" (9:3).
6. And sometimes, as we have seen in the experience Job, suffering may have a hidden purpose in the plan of God that may never be known to the one enduring the trial (Job 1:6-2:10).

When suffering comes, it is only natural for us to ask, "Why?" Perhaps God, through His Word, will make the answer known. Perhaps He will not. But we must move beyond our initial response of "Why?" and seek the spiritual lessons God might be teaching us through our personal trial. We need to move beyond the "Why?" to the "What?" What does God want to accomplish and teach me through this experience?

The Bible offers further directions for those who suffer:

1. Recognize God's sovereignty over the situation, trusting the faithful Creator to do what is right (Romans 8:28; 1 Peter 4:16).
2. Rejoice in the trial (James 1:3), thanking Him in the midst of the situation (1 Thessalonians 5:18).
3. Don't be surprised or ashamed when suffering for the sake of your personal faith (1 Peter 4:12, 16).

4. Follow Jesus' example of patient endurance when suffering unjustly (1 Peter 2:19-21).

Suffering can bear fruit in our lives if we respond to it biblically. A proper response to suffering will produce perseverance, maturity, proven character, and godliness (Romans 5:3-5; James 1:3-4; 2 Corinthians 4:8-10).

Even as wise and successful men and women, we may face suffering that is beyond explanation. We wonder why, but no answer is forthcoming. In such a situation we must remember that God is in control. We don't need to know why if we know God. He has not seen fit to give us a reason for everything He does, but the Book of Job sets forth a God so great that no answer is needed.

Del and Ellen, the couple with the Down's syndrome baby mentioned earlier, shared their triumphant response to what would otherwise be considered a tragic situation:

> When we first learned of David's condition, we felt so helpless and wondered how we could handle such a thing, especially in a foreign country. All the inevitable questions about ourselves and about God came flooding into our minds, but as we went to the Word many verses took on special meaning for us. Two principles in particular have been especially helpful in beginning to accept and to adjust to this new circumstance in our lives.
>
> *First*, God made David just as he is and gave him to us to love and care for, and He never makes mistakes. He is God's unique gift to us and we give thanks to Him Who knows what is best for us.
>
> *Second*, we may never know why God made our child this way, for His ways are deep, unfathomable, unsearchable, and our minds are so very finite (Romans 11:32). When Jesus was questioned about why a certain man was born blind, He replied, "That the work of God might be displayed in his life." Our hope and prayer is that

God might show His works in David's life and thus bring glory to Himself.

Don't be surprised by suffering! Bad things do happen to God's people. Not even the wise and successful are shielded from the tragedy and misfortune associated with living in a fallen, sinful world. But there is a way to handle suffering when it comes our way.

Del and Ellen were successful in dealing with their suffering—not because they understood the reason for it, but because they *knew* God. And when people know God, He gives them sufficient grace to live with unanswered questions. That's living successfully in a broken and messed up world!

Study and Review Questions

1. What biblical evidence is there that Job's monumental suffering was not due to personal sin?
2. How is it encouraging to know that Satan had to receive permission from God before bringing calamity into Job's life?
3. What was the major problem with the view on suffering presented by Job's three friends?
4. How did Elihu, the young man, explain Job's suffering? What evidence is there that he was on the right track?
5. When the Lord spoke to Job (chapters 38-41), He did not even mention Job's suffering. How did God help Job deal with his suffering?
6. What are a few of the reasons Christians might suffer?
7. Reflect on an experience when you have suffered. How did you respond? How will you respond the next time you experience suffering?

Chapter 3
COPING WITH LIFE'S FRUSTRATIONS

Successful people are free from the mundane frustrations of life. Right? Wrong! Successful people face the same frustrations that confront us all—traffic jams, misplaced eyeglasses, and greener-than-grass dandelions in the front lawn. But those who have discovered God's key to success (Ecclesiastes 10:10) have learned to cope with life's frustrations. It all begins with our attitude.

Life: To Enjoy or Tolerate?
Do you really enjoy living? Or do the frustrations of daily life get you down? Do you take time each day to laugh with friends, fellowship at the table, or enjoy a quiet evening walk? Or do you face life with a stoic determination to endure and "bear up" under the circumstances until you breathe your last breath. "Yes, I'll hang in there," straitlaced, sober and sad.

Should God's people take time out for leisure and the enjoyments of life? Such activities might be considered "worldly." Like many personalities of the past, perhaps you feel a twinge of guilt when you spend time and money on pursuits that are pleasure or leisure oriented. Such a man was Simon Stylites.

Saint Simeon, surnamed *Stylites* (from the Greek word for "pillar"), lived in Syria in the fourth century A.D. He looked with disdain upon the pleasurable things of life. Simeon was just thirteen years old when he entered a monastery near Antioch to devote himself to rigid exercises of self-mortification and abstinence.

Simeon was an ascetic. He deprived himself of any pleasure in life or social interaction. For Simeon, this was *victorious* Christian living. In order to isolate himself further, Simeon began living on the top of a stone column which was raised from six to twelve, and eventually to thirty-six feet in height.

At the top of the pillar was a small platform three feet in diameter surrounded by a handrail. There Simeon spent the rest of his life. There was no room to lie down on the platform, so he stood all day and night, enduring all kinds of wind and weather.

Simeon spent his nights in constant prayer, spreading his hands and bowing so low that his forehead almost touched his toes. He took only one scanty meal a week and fasted throughout the season of Lent—a period of forty days!

Simeon died on September 1, A.D. 460, after thirty-seven years on his pillar. He was buried in Antioch and his pillar was later enclosed by a chapel and monastery.

Some fun, huh? Is this what abundant life (John 10:10) is all about? Are we simply to tolerate life and its frustrations until the bitter end? Or is there an alternative for those seeking to live wisely?

In the frequently misunderstood Book of Ecclesiastes, Solomon addressed this issue. There he revealed God's solution to coping with life's inevitable frustrations. If you have ever experienced frustration in your work, family or career, wise old King Solomon offers some life-changing counsel.

Exploring Ecclesiastes

While Solomon is not clearly identified as the author, he is the most likely person to have written the book. This is suggested by the author's royalty (1:1), unrivaled wisdom (1:16), unequaled wealth (2:7), opportunities for pleasure (2:3), and extensive building activities (2:4-6). Jewish tradition clearly identifies Solomon as the author of the book.

The Hebrew title, Qohelet means "one who convenes and speaks at an assembly," suggesting the circumstances of the book's composition. The Book of Ecclesiastes is apparently the record of Solomon's teaching given at an assembly of the wise sometime during the latter days of his life. Drawing upon his great wisdom and experience, Solomon dispensed some very practical instruction to God's people.

One popular interpretation of Ecclesiastes is presented in the notes of the *New Scofield Reference Bible*:

> Ecclesiastes is the book of man "under the sun" reasoning about life. The philosophy it sets forth, which makes no claim to revelation but which inspiration records for our instruction, represents the world-view of one of the wisest men.[4]

This view suggests that Ecclesiastes contains the best reasoning about life that man can produce. But we ask, "If the book merely contains the reasons of a wise man, what guarantee is there that they are true?

A more consistent approach to Ecclesiasts has been suggested by a British scholar, J. Stafford Wright.[5] He believes that the book provides the answer to dealing with life's frustrations.

According to Wright, Ecclesiastes demonstrates that it is utterly futile to assimilate all the riddles and paradoxes of life. There is no need to frustrate ourselves. God simply has not revealed the answers to all of life's inconsistencies. But God has shown us that in spite of the futility of trying to put all of life together, we can live by faith and use this one opportunity to serve God and enjoy life to the fullest. An exploration of Ecclesiastes will validate this approach. In this ancient book we discover the key to coping with life's frustrations.

Facing the Frustrations of Life

In the first section of Ecclesiastes (1:1-2:23), Solomon reflected on the fact that life is often frustrating. He acknowledged the futility of trying to resolve all the dilemmas and frustrations of life.

Solomon's Thesis (1:1). Solomon began by setting forth his thesis of the utter futility of all things. "Vanity of vanities," said Solomon, "vanity of vanities! All is vanity"

---

[4] *The New Scofield Reference Bible*, 1967 ed., 696.

[5] J. Stafford Wright, "The Interpretation of Ecclesiastes," *Evangelical Quarterly* 18 (1946): 18-34.

(1:2). The expression "vanity of vanities" can be literally translated, "vapor of vapors" and means "thinnest of vapors."

Life with its activities is much like the morning mist that hangs over a mountain lake and vanishes with the first rays of the sun. As we consider our day, what did we really accomplish? Is there any point to it all? What is the ultimate benefit of our hard work? Life is over all too quickly and what we accomplish often seems insignificant. Solomon's thesis accords well with Paul's teaching that all creation is subject to futility because of sin (Romans 8:20-22).

The Illustrations (1:3-11). Solomon went on to provide a number of illustrations of his thesis. Life is futile because there is no guarantee of positive benefit for our work on this earth. "What advantage does man have in all his work which he does under the sun?" (1:3). Hard work is sometimes not remunerated nor even appreciated. The expression "under the sun" is a figure of speech in which the location is described instead of being named. It is used repeatedly in Ecclesiastes to refer to "the earth" where people live. Solomon is not reflecting on "life without God." He is simply describing life as we experience it here on earth.

Solomon called attention to the transitory nature of man's existence. "A generation goes and a generation comes, but the earth remains forever" (1:4). People come and go from earth with little lasting or significant effect. Solomon reminds us of how creation follows endless, changeless cycles and he concludes that there is a monotonous futility in all things (1:5-8). The future will just repeat the past, and the past will inevitably be forgotten.

Who among us cannot identify with Solomon's thesis? Seasons come and go, but life's labors continue. And who appreciates the effort expended? What is the ultimate benefit of all our labor and toil?

I work hard in the spring planting my vegetable garden. But the seeds sometimes rot in the ground and my little cucumber plants wither and die for no apparent reason. My tomatoes finally appear in August, but fail to ripen before being split by the rain of early fall. My two largest pumpkins turn yellow and then rot on the vine. How frustrating! What futility!

I enter my home where my grandchildren are visiting. Just a half hour ago I picked up their toys from the front room and placed the children's books back on the shelf where they belong. I had straightened the magazines on the coffee table and the pillows on the sofa. But during my thirty-minute sojourn in my garage, disaster struck! My toddler grandson has tipped over a potted plan and has a mouth full of leaves. My older grandson has his Lego blocks spread out on the rug and my granddaughter has sixteen story books distributed around the sofa.

While "Grammy" is taking this in stride, I am not so easy going. "Vanity of vanities!" I exclaim. I agree with Solomon. There is a frustrating futility that characterizes much of life on planet earth.

Searching for a Solution (1:12-2:23). How are we to cope with life's frustrations? Can we maintain our sanity in an insane world? With his great resources and wealth, Solomon explored a number of possible solutions.

Solomon attempted to find relief from life's frustrations by focusing on his career (1:14). Perhaps you have tried that too! But in spite of his significant royal responsibilities, Solomon found that much of his labor was merely futile activity. Where could he find some lasting benefit and value? Using his unlimited resources, Solomon began to experiment and search for meaning in life. He found through personal experience that pleasure (2:1), achievements (2:4-6), possessions and wealth (2:7-8), and great fame (2:9), all failed to bring him enduring satisfaction.

In the end, Solomon concluded, "Thus I considered all my activities which my hands had done and the labor which I had exerted, and behold all was vanity and striving after wind and there was no profit under the sun" (2:11).

We can all identify in some way with Solomon's dilemma. Facing a life of futility and frustration can be most discouraging. Is it possible to keep one's sanity in this situation? Does God's wisdom provide us with the key to success in dealing with frustration?

After a long life of struggling with these issues, Solomon commends to us a prescription for dealing with life's inevitable frustrations.

Enjoying Life as A Gift from God

Having contemplated the utter futility of life, Solomon presents his divinely inspired solution. Rather than chafe under the frustrations and futilities of life, Solomon counsels that we should enjoy to the fullest the life God has given us, recognizing it as His special gift. "Don't fret about matters over which you have no control. Instead, enjoy life!" This prescription for dealing with life's frustrations is recorded seven times in Ecclesiastes 2:24-12:7.

Considering the Counsel (2:24-26). Solomon advised, "There is nothing better for a man than to eat and drink and tell himself that his labor is good. This also I have seen, that it is from the hand of God" (2:24). When Solomon said, "there is nothing better," he is not demeaning his own counsel. He is using a literary device that is the opposite of hyperbole (exaggeration for the sake of emphasis). Here and throughout the book Solomon uses *understatement* for the sake of emphasis. The phrase, "there is nothing better," means, "the best thing is...." A few years ago teenagers used a similar device when they described their favorite things as "bad."

The often repeated phrase "eat and drink" is a Hebrew expression for enjoying life (Matthew 11:18-19). Eating and drinking were an important part of any festive celebration. Solomon is saying, "Enjoy life! Live every day like a festival!"

The counsel to "enjoy life" is emphasized by the words *joy* and *rejoice*. They appear seventeen times in

Ecclesiastes. In later Judaism, Ecclesiastes was read on the third day of the Feast of Tabernacles (*Sukkot*), a thanksgiving or harvest festival.

Solomon's solution to the paradoxes and frustrations of life has special application for the people of God. He adds, "For who can eat and who can have enjoyment without Him?" (2:25). Knowing God is the key to enjoying life to the fullest and appreciating its blessings as divinely bestowed gifts.

In the living room of my home hangs an oil painting of some lovely Texas bluebonnets. Anyone could appreciate the artistry and colors in that painting, but I can appreciate them considerably more because I met the artist when I purchased the painting. In the same way, believers have a much greater capacity to enjoy the artistry and beauty of God's creation because they *know* the Creator.

We cannot deny the existence of frustrations, paradoxes, and inconsistencies in life. But God has given believers the ability and opportunity to enjoy life in spite of these difficulties. In fact, the enjoyment of life is the key to maintaining one's sanity and good humor in the face of life's perplexities.

The solution offered by Solomon is capsulized in the refrain, "Eat, drink and be happy, for this is the gift of God" (2:24; 3:12-13; 3:22; 5:18-20; 8:15; 9:7-9; 11:9). This statement is the theme of Ecclesiastes. It was Solomon's way of emphasizing that there is no real contradiction between enjoying life to the fullest and living a life of obedience to God. The Lord clearly intended for the godly person to do both.

Epicurean Sensualism. Some have mistakenly identified Solomon's counsel with that of the Epicurean sensualists, "Let us eat, drink, and be merry, for tomorrow we die." This philosophy originated with Epicurus (341-270 B.C.), a Greek philosopher of Athens. He condemned excess and commended a simple mode of life. Epicurus viewed happiness and the avoidance of pain as the chief ends of life.

His philosophy of life was later twisted into an approach to life in which self-indulgent pleasure-seeking was viewed as the only good. Hedonism (from the Greek word *hedone*, "delight") is really a perversion of Epicurean teaching. Epicurus said, "Avoid life and its pains by retiring from the world." The Hedonist said, "Exploit life by indulging in its sensual pleasures." Solomon rejected by extremes. He said, "Eat, drink and be happy, for life is a gift from God."

Elaborating the Dimensions. Throughout the rest of Ecclesiastes, Solomon repeated his prescription for coping with frustration, adding some further dimensions to his counsel, "Enjoy life."

1. *Do good in one's lifetime (3:12-13).* Life is not designed by God to consist simply of an eternal pursuit of pleasure. Rather, we are to give ourselves to meaningful activity. As God's people, our work of evangelism, discipleship and social justice is eternally significant and meaningful. We can find joy in doing things that count for eternity.

2. *Find fulfillment in one's labor (5:18-19).* Life's opportunities are a divine gift, said Solomon. Such fulfillment is the godly person's inheritance or reward this side of heaven. Solomon was suggesting that the wise man or woman will have a positive attitude toward work. In spite of the futilities, work is a divinely ordained opportunity for meaningful expression.

3. *Enjoy life's blessings today (9:7-8).* In the midst of a busy week and a frustrating schedule we find ourselves saying, "When Friday comes, I'm going to take a break and enjoy myself." Solomon advised, "Don't save your best white clothes and fragrant body oil just for festivals" (9:8). Rather, enjoy each day as you would a festival. We ought not look for tomorrow to find the relief we need today. The key to coping with life's frustrations is to find enjoyment in *each* day.

4. *Take daily delight in your marriage (9:9).* Solomon commended the joys of marriage as a source of consolation and encouragement in times of frustration or difficulty. He was saying, "Don't let the frustrations and futilities of life prevent you from enjoying pleasant times daily with your life's companion." It is important for couples to plan to spend time together daily. Even just a few minutes of conversation over a cup of coffee or hot chocolate provides an opportunity to share the events of the day and enjoy the blessing of companionship.

5. *Follow the directions of your heart (11:9).* In his last exhortation to enjoy life, Solomon encourages us to follow the impulses of our heart and the desires of our eyes. Solomon was certainly not encouraging indulgence in sinful pleasures. The word *impulses* would be better translated "ways." Solomon was saying, "Follow the ways or directions placed in your heart by God." It is not God's pattern to lead us against our will or consecrated desire. He will lead us *through* our will and desires into His perfect plan. If we delight in the Lord, His desires for us will become our desires (Psalm 37:4).

Enjoying Life on a Budget. Solomon has been telling his readers to "enjoy life." Now you might be wondering, "How can I do that on a limited budget?"

Having spent seven years as a graduate school student, I have become something of an expert on enjoying life inexpensively. Money is not the key to happiness and joy. We can learn to appreciate the simple things of life. Prime rib is delicious, but this might be a rare treat if you are living on a limited budget. Yet almost everyone can appreciate and enjoy a good, mustard doused hotdog!

There are many brief opportunities to enjoy life throughout the day. One can find such moments during daily devotions, as the dawn breaks during a morning run, as one savors the last drops from a glass of orange juice, kisses their wife or husband good-bye, walks in the park, enjoys an evening with friends or family, or gazes at a harvest moon with one's sweetheart. These moments give us reasons to say, "Thank you, Lord, for this wonderful day."

Each day will have its challenges and frustrations. But if we follow Solomon's wise counsel, we can enjoy many special moments during the day as gifts and blessings from God.

Keeping the Balance

According to Solomon, the wisest of the Wisdom teachers, much of life on this earth seems futile and frustrating. Solomon sought a solution to some of the perplexities and riddles he faced, but found none. In the end, he commended the enjoyment of life as a divinely ordained prescription for dealing with life's frustrations.

In the closing verses of Ecclesiastes, Solomon emphasized an important aspect of the solution he recommended. He has encouraged us to enjoy life. At the same time, he reminds us of our accountability before God. Fearing God and obeying His Word are our ultimate responsibilities (12:13-14).

The futility of life has not been resolved. But Solomon has told us how to live righteously and joyously on earth anyway. He has encouraged us to enjoy life as a divine gift, while living with an awareness of our ethical responsibilities.

The life God ordained for each of us often seems futile and frustrating. But we need not despair. We can live day by day seeking to obey and glorify God in the midst of perplexing circumstances. In this daily service for God we will find great enjoyment.

We need not climb up on a pillar like Simeon Stylites to avoid the problems and pains of life. Instead, we can enjoy God's gift of life to the fullest. But so doing we will find the fulfillment and blessing that enables us to cope with the inevitable frustrations of life.

Study and Review Questions

1. What was Solomon's major thesis in Ecclesiastes? What is the meaning of the words, *vanity of vanities?*
2. Does Solomon's thesis make sense to you? In what way have you also experienced the futilities of life?
3. What solution does Solomon offer for dealing with life's frustrations? Explain Solomon's counsel in Ecclesiasts 2:24.
4. How does Solomon's solution to life's frustrations differ from that of the Epicureans and Hedonists?
5. How do Solomon's words in the epilogue of Ecclesiastes (12:8-14) enable believers to better understand his counsel?
6. What steps can you take to begin enjoying life more this week?

Chapter 4
MAINTAINING SEXUAL PURITY

Rarely does a month go by that I do not learn of someone whose life and reputation have been tarnished by sexual impropriety. Sadly, many of these people are professing Christians. Evangelist Luis Palau has declared, "More of my fellow evangelists have wrecked their lives because of sexual temptation than for any other reason." Countless marriages have been destroyed and lives shattered by sexual misconduct.

Now some of us might be saying, "That's awful! But it surely wouldn't happen to me." Yet many well-intentioned people are overcome by temptation. They are successful in their career and ministry, but have not applied the principles of wisdom to their moral conduct. Unexpected disaster lurks on their horizon.

A Lack of Vigilance

On the night of December 6, 1941, just twelve hours before the Japanese attack on Pearl Harbor, Admiral Kimmel, commander in chief of the Pacific Fleet, attended a dinner party with a number of important naval commanders and their wives. One woman, the wife of Admiral Halsey, said she was certain that the Japanese were going to attack. Everyone at the party thought she was crazy. Twelve hours later, on a sleepy Sunday morning, Japanese warplanes began bombing Pearl Harbor.

At a naval inquiry in 1944, Admiral Leary spoke of the complacency at the daily conferences held by Admiral Kimmel during the weeks preceding the attack. When asked whether any thought had been given to the possibility of a surprise attack by the Japanese, he said, "We all felt that the contingency was remote." The same attitude was epitomized in testimony given by Captain Earle, Chief of Staff, Fourteenth Naval District, "We all felt that it couldn't happen here."

The consistent testimony given by Admiral Kimmel's advisers was that they acted on the basis of an unwarranted feeling of immunity from attack. Their lack of vigilance and preparedness led them down the pathway to unexpected disaster.

Many people have an unwarranted feeling of immunity from attack in the area of sexual purity. If this is true in your case, you may be unwittingly heading for disaster.

Sex is one of the best and most beautiful gifts God has been pleased to give men and women. But like the forbidden fruit in the Garden of Eden, people sometimes take the best gifts of God and use them prematurely and in ways they were not intended. By indulging in sexual relations outside of marriage, we tarnish one of God's best gifts.

Solomon's Encouragement Toward Sexual Purity
The Song of Solomon sets forth the purity and beauty of married love and its physical expression. The Song has a special message for married couples but it also has an important lesson for those who are single.

In chapter 2 the Shulammite maiden expresses her love for her husband Solomon and her desire for sexual intimacies (2:3-6). But then she adds a warning to the "daughters of Jerusalem" (2:7). These young, unmarried girls were court maidens or ladies in waiting. They were not actually present in the royal couple's bedroom, but are referred to here in a literary sense for the purpose of instructing the reader. Verse 7, then, is an aside, or a parenthesis, which gives balance to the emphasis on the physical aspect of love found in the Song.

The Shulammite maiden, Solomon's bride, gives a solemn warning to the unmarried maidens. "I adjure you, O daughters of Jerusalem, by the gazelles or the hinds of the field." Instead of invoking the name of God in her appeal for an oath of purity, the Shulammite invokes the existence of the lovely little deer so common in ancient Israel. The gazelle and the hind (a female deer), are noted for their elegance in form and movement.

By the existence of these graceful deer, the maidens are admonished that they "not arouse or awaken love until it pleases." The word *awaken* is used here for the stirring up of sexual desires. Solomon's bride is warning the young unmarried women in the court that they not awaken the *physical expression* of love—sexual passion—prematurely. The phrase, "until it pleases," means "until it is appropriate."

This warning against premarital and extramarital sex is repeated three times in the Song of Solomon (2:7; 3:5; 8:4). Solomon's bride is essentially saying, "The physical expression of love in marriage is a beautiful experience, but it's also a powerful force. So don't fan the flames of sexual passion prematurely. Recognize that sex has its proper place in the marriage union. It is in the God-ordained relationship of marriage that the physical expression of love will be blessed."

The Shulammite maiden's warning is quite in keeping with God's statement in Genesis 2:24 concerning marriage as He ordained it. Here marriage is seen to involve three main elements: (1) a *public act* by which the couple announces their plans to "leave" their parents and establish a new family unit, (2) a *permanent bond* to which the two commit themselves as they "cleave" to one another, and (3) a *physical embrace* in which the marriage union is consummated as the couple becomes "one flesh."

The divine order revealed in Genesis 2:24 is significant. First, there is the "leaving" and "cleaving" and *then* "becoming one flesh." The sexual union does not precede the establishment of the marriage relationship. God clearly designed sexual intercourse for marriage. To indulge oneself outside the context of marriage is to violate the divine order and leads to unnecessary guilt, relationship complications, and deep regret.

Some people argue these days that sexual desire is just as natural as wanting a drink of water, and to deny this desire leaves a person totally unfulfilled. Jim Frantz, one of my single students, addressed this problem in a term paper. He wrote:

47

Sexual fulfillment can only achieve its highest potential when both partners can completely trust each other for emotional security. It is only through marriage that this security can be established.

Instead of seeing God's restrictions on sexual expression as being unfair and puritanical, I, as a single person, can accept how He has created me as someone with sexual feelings that do not require expression outside of marriage. Just because God designed sex to be an extremely pleasurable experience does not mean it must be satisfied. My non-expression of my sexual nature in no way lessens my "manhood" or makes me an unfulfilled person.

Jim recognizes that God made sex for marriage and that He will bless it only in that context.

While sex is a fulfilling experience between two married people, it is not the only way for us to find fulfillment. Paul wrote of the fulfillment that can be found in serving Christ (1 Corinthians 7:25-35). Certainly no one would argue that Jesus, who lived His life as a single person, lacked fulfillment.

Solomon's Warnings Against Sexual Promiscuity
Sexual promiscuity is one of the most effective tools Satan uses to destroy the lives and ministries of God's people. Yet this need not be the case for you. In the Book of Proverbs, God sets forth some warnings that will enable Spirit-controlled believers to avoid the sin and sadness of sexual immorality.

The Character of the Promiscuous. I attended a Bible study breakfast with one of my students who has a ministry to truck drivers. We met at a truck stop café and enjoyed a good time of fellowship and Bible study. Later that afternoon, Tom was in my office talking about the study. "Did you notice that woman in the restaurant?" he asked. I had noticed her. I had assumed the woman was a trucker's wife. "She's a prostitute," Tom said. "You can tell by her clothes, by the way she was acting around the men in the restaurant, and by the way they were following her with their eyes."

Perhaps I'm a bit naïve when it comes to the ways of the promiscuous. But I shouldn't be. We ought to be able to identify a promiscuous person so we won't be caught off guard and be drawn into an illicit relationship.

In Proverbs, Solomon identifies some of the characteristics of a "strange woman." She is called "strange" (literally, a "foreigner") because she is outside the circle of a man's appropriate relationships. Speaking from the viewpoint of a man, Solomon describes a loose woman. The same characteristics could help identify a promiscuous man.

1. *The promiscuous person is a flatterer (2:16; 5:3; 6:24).* A flatterer offers insincere compliments and praise for the purpose of swaying another person. The promiscuous woman flatters her potential lover into thinking that he is the sole subject of her affections. "I have come out to meet you, to seek your presence earnestly, and I have found you" (7:15). Her words are enticing as honey and smoother than oil (5:3). Beware of insincere compliments, especially when their focus is on the physical. Such compliments are instruments of seduction.

2. *The promiscuous person is unfaithful (2:17).* Solomon said that the adulterous "leaves the companion of her youth." This unfaithfulness often begins in the thoughts and emotions. Beware of the married person who publicly criticizes his or her spouse. This expresses a lack of commitment and often indicates that the person is seeking emotional support elsewhere.

3. *The promiscuous person is often a backslider (2:17b).* Solomon said that the "adulteress "forgets the covenant of her God." This may be a reference to the marriage covenant (Malachi 2:14) or God's covenant with Israel—including the obligations of the seventh commandment (Exodus 20:14). The point is that she has a religious background, but is not walking with the Lord. A professing Christian husband left his wife for another woman. When he returned home to pick up his belongings he grabbed his Bible and told his wife, "Well, at least she is a Christian." Beware of personal involvement with a backslider. A relationship with such a person will not contribute to your spiritual wellbeing.

4. *The promiscuous person is unstable (5:6).* Promiscuous people are restless, flitting around from interest to interest without any lasting commitment. They are always looking for a "piece of the action." Be cautious in dealing with a person who has unstable tendencies.

5. *The Promiscuous person focuses on the physical (6:25; 7:10).* The harlot wears clothing that accentuates the physical body. Suggestive attire may indicate that a man or a woman is "on the prowl." Solomon warned, "Do not desire her beauty in your heart, nor let her catch you with her eyelids" (6:25). Solomon is not suggesting that physical beauty is not to be appreciated in the right context (Song of Solomon 5:1-6). Rather, he is cautioning us not to focus on the physical attractiveness of someone with whom we are not married. A wise man won't make a fuss over the attractiveness of his secretary. He will compliment her for how well she performs her work, not for how nice she looks in her cashmere sweater.

6. *The promiscuous person is a gadabout (7:11).* Solomon said of the adulteress, "She is boisterous and rebellious; her feet do not remain at home." The promiscuous chafe under family responsibility and moral restraint. They are busy minding everyone's else's business instead of tending to their own family obligations.

7. *The promiscuous person is a schemer (6:26; 23:28).* Solomon likened the adulteress to a wild animal stalking its victim. She "lurks as a robber" (23:28) and "hunts for the precious life" (6:26). The promiscuous person has a strategy to conquer his or her victim. Beware of a schemer, especially when the scheme appears to involve *you!*

8. *The promiscuous person denies the sinfulness of sin (30:20).* The adulteress "eats and wipes her mouth and says, 'I have done no wrong.'" Someone has said that having sex is no different than having a sandwich or drinking a glass of water. It meets a normal, physical need. But calling sexual promiscuity "right" does not make it so. This is just an attempt to soothe the guilt feelings that come from knowingly violating God's standards.

The Encounter with the Promiscuous. Solomon provides us with an eyewitness account of a young man's encounter with an adulteress (Proverbs 7:6-27). This passage dramatizes Solomon's warning against adultery and illustrates how one succumbs to the temptations of a promiscuous person.

Looking out the window, Solomon observed a naïve, young man flirting with temptation. Aimless, with time on his hands, he walks by the house of the adulteress (7:8-9). He isn't really planning an illicit relationship, but has placed himself in the midst of an enticing situation. The adulteress takes over from there.

She comes out to meet the young man. Her attire ("dressed as a harlot") reveals the seductive nature of her activities (7:10). She is likened to a preying animal that "lurks" after its victim (7:12). She uses a close embrace and kisses to elicit a sensual response from her potential lover (7:13). With flattery, she deceives the young man into thinking that he is the special subject of her affections (7:15). She then proceeds with a sensuous appeal, describing her bedroom, which she has prepared for this special occasion of lovemaking (7:16-17). Finally, the invitation, "Come, let us drink our fill of love until morning; let us delight ourselves with caresses" (7:18). She assures the young man that he won't get caught. Her husband is away on business and is not expected to return for many days (7:19-20).

Solomon described the young man going off with the adulteress, having succumbed to her seduction. He follows her as an ox goes to the slaughter (7:22). Little does this naïve fool realize the peril of his situation. Carried away by sensual desires, he lays hold of a momentary thrill at the cost of his very life. Solomon warned that the house of the adulteress is "the way of *Sheol* [Hebrew for "pit" or "grave"], descending to the chambers of death" (7:27). To be successful in life, we must learn a lesson from the victims of the promiscuous woman and avoid her paths.

The Judgment on the Promiscuous. Solomon pointed out that it is impossible to engage in sexual immorality without suffering devastating consequences (Proverbs 6:25-31). Solomon is saying in essence, "You can't carry fire in your arms without igniting your clothes or walk on hot coals without burning your feet. So you cannot commit adultery and expect to escape injury" (6:27-29). This truth is confirmed in the New Testament, "Let marriage be held in honor among all, and let the marriage bed be undefiled; for fornicators and adulterers God will judge" (Hebrews 13:4).

Concerning the adulterer, Solomon said, "Wounds and disgrace he will find, and his reproach will not be blotted out" (Proverbs 6:33). The "wounds" may refer either to the bodily injury inflicted by the outraged husband or the physical discipline brought on by the Lord (Hebrew 12:5-11). The "disgrace" refers to the injury done to one's reputation. Sexual promiscuity brings wounds that take a long time to heal and does grave damage to one's honor and reputation.

Solomon was not suggesting, of course, that sexual immorality is an unpardonable sin. Jesus paid the penalty for *all* sin by His sacrificial death on the cross. We understand clearly that a person can be forgiven and cleansed from any sin of the past (1 John 1:9). But Solomon was issuing a stern warning. Sexual promiscuity is not to be taken lightly. The grievous consequences of sexual immorality far outweigh the momentary pleasure found in an illicit relationship.

Maintaining Sexual Purity

It's not impossible. Whether married or single, a man or woman can maintain sexual purity and avoid the devastating consequences of immorality. People don't really *fall* into immorality. They slip into it a little by little—a compromise here, a wandering thought there, a greater tolerance for sexual innuendo and sensual appeal. When the major slipup occurs, it is usually the result of a long history of minor, moral concessions.

But it doesn't have to happen that way. Adultery is avoidable. After hearing about a friend's marital unfaithfulness, my wife and I had a serious conversation about how we could avoid such a disaster in our own marriage. We developed the following list of guidelines which have proven effective in helping us as a couple steer clear of immoral situations. I share this with you as a prescription for marital faithfulness.

We never say, "It can't happen to me." To think that we are somehow immune to sexual sin is to deceive ourselves and give temptation a chance to take us by surprise. Remember the lack of vigilance that preceded the attack on Pearl Harbor? Anyone can fall prey to sexual immorality. It is best to be on guard against that possibility.

We plan our response to temptation beforehand. When anticipating a tempting situation, we plan how we are going to handle it. A business or ministry trip may afford opportunities for sexual temptation, so Nancy and I plan to make contact by phone every evening we are separated. When I am away from home, I take plenty of reading material to keep me occupied in the evenings when temptation is prone to strike.

We are diligent to control our thought life. Paul encouraged the Philippians to think on those things that are right, pure, and lovely (Philippians 4:8). Immorality begins in the mind. When we find ourselves beginning to fantasize an inappropriate relationship, we refocus on Jesus (Hebrews 12:1-2) and our marriage commitment to each other. We are alert to the dangers of subjecting our minds to sexually stimulating films, books or conversations. These may stir desires that lead to immoral activities.

We are available to each other for intimate times. Proverbs encourages married couples to delight themselves in the physical relationship that God designed for marriage (Proverbs 5:18-19). We take time to develop and enrich our marital intimacy by scheduling special overnight trips together away from the distractions of children and housework. We have found that if we focus our affections on the person God has given us in marriage, we won't be as likely to become interested in someone else.

We speak openly of our love and commitment for each other. It is important to let our friends and acquaintances know where we stand in terms of marital commitment. When I meet an attractive woman on a trip or at a conference, it isn't long before I show her pictures of my wife and family. This not only helps us get acquainted, but it also sets the perimeters of the relationship.

We guard our conversation. We are alert to the dangers of deeply personal and intimate conversations with someone of the opposite sex. Confiding with someone about our marriage or family issues may lead to an emotional involvement. It is wiser to discuss such matters with each other or seek professional help from our pastor or counselor.

We avoid enticing opportunities. Nancy and I guard against being maneuvered into situations that might lead to sexual temptation. A phone call or business appointment may have a hidden agenda. We know our own limits and set boundaries to avoid situations that may lead to a tempting opportunity.

We are aware of the feelings that touching can generate. Hugs, kisses, and caresses among family members reinforce the loving atmosphere of the home. While a hug or kiss on the cheek may have their place among close friends, physical contact with members of the opposite sex can stimulate sexual arousal. I am sure that the beautiful wife of one of my colleagues was not aware of the shot of adrenaline that surged through my veins when she gently placed her hand on my arm during a conversation at a Christmas party. Many people are not aware of the arousal they can cause by gentle, mostly friendly, touch. As a married couple, we are careful to avoid stimulating desires in others that cannot be legitimately satisfied.

We are accountable to someone outside our marriage. We have found that accountability to someone outside of marriage is an essential key to keeping pure and faithful in our marriage. This is especially true when one is struggling with the temptation of pornography or an illicit relationship. Reporting regularly to an accountability partner on our spiritual condition helps us to get back on track before we turn aside and follow the path of temptation and sin.

We recognize that the delights of illicit sex are fantasy and illusion. The power of temptation is the illusion that sin can make us happier than God can. If you find yourself fantasizing about illicit sex, take it the next step. Fantasize the day *after* illicit sex when you are trying to cover your tracks with lies. Fantasize the day when your sin is exposed. Fantasize the day when you have to explain to your children the loss of your job or your ministry. The fantasy of illicit sex will always exceed the pleasure of the reality. It is one of Satan's best strategies to destroy marriages.

We remember that God always provides a way of escape (1 Corinthians 10:13). Sexual sin brings devastating consequences to a marriage. But it doesn't have to happen to you. By following the example of Joseph (Genesis 39:12) and the exhortation of Paul (2 Timothy 2:22), sexual sin can be avoided. God promises to provide a "way of escape" (1 Cor. 10:13) so that we need not fall victim to sin.

The Way to Success

During his seminary days, a friend of mine worked for a furniture store, making deliveries. One day he had to deliver a bed to the apartment of an attractive young woman. After he put the bed and mattress in place, she looked into his eyes and brazenly said, "Wouldn't you like to be the first to try it with me?" Temptation strikes!

Before my friend could give the opportunity a second thought, he said, "No, thanks," and darted out the door. By taking "the way of escape" (1 Corinthians 10:13), he was successful in avoiding the burden of guilt and painful consequences of illicit sexual activity. And he honored God by maintaining his sexual purity. By God's power and enablement, we can too!

Study and Review Questions

1. What important message does the Song of Solomon have for single people? Express the key thought in your own words (2:7; 3:5; 8:4).
2. What does Genesis 2:24 reveal about God's plan for marriage? What is the divinely ordained context for the expression of the sexual union?
3. Proverbs describes the characteristics of the promiscuous person. Which of these characteristics are easily observable? Which are subtle and appear only with time and familiarity?
4. In Proverbs 7:6-27, Solomon described the encounter of a naïve youth with an adulteress. Have the ways of the promiscuous changed any since Solomon's time? Is there anything you would add to Solomon's description?
5. According to Solomon, what are the inevitable consequences of sexual immorality? Is sexual sin unpardonable? How can you help someone to deal with sexual sin of the past (1 John 1:9)?
6. What is your strategy for maintaining sexual purity? What guidelines could you add to the ones offered here?

Chapter 5
SUCCEEDING AT WORK

What was your first paying job? It may have been baby-sitting or mowing the neighbor's lawn. We all remember the impressions that first work experience left with us.

I was eleven years old when my family traveled by train to Georgia, where we spent the summer with my grandparents. A few days after our arrival, I was awakened early in the morning by my uncle Otis. "Come on," he said, "I've got a job for you!"

After a breakfast of grits and cinnamon toast, my uncle took me to his fruit stand at the farmer's market. There I spent the rest of the summer earning $1.50 a day selling fresh, Georgia peaches, cantaloupes, and watermelons. I loved the work and felt a sense of pride over the responsibility I had been entrusted with. Thus began a career that has included picking beans, harvesting blueberries, making plywood, shoveling asphalt, canning beets, driving a school bus, preaching, writing, and teaching the Bible. And it all started at a Georgia fruit stand.

Does work give you a sense of accomplishment, satisfaction, and fulfillment? Or does the mere word "work" fill you with thoughts of dread, anxiety, and gloom? Do you enjoy work, or do you hate it?

For most adults and many young people, work is a big part of their day. They drive trucks, teach school, sell insurance, build houses, and run businesses. Some work at home caring for children and keeping house. Others work at an office, answering phones, filling out reports, and responding to email. Most people work eight hours a day, five days a week, fifty weeks out of the year until they retire around the age of sixty-five or sixty-six.

Most of our waking hours are somehow associated with work—preparing for it, driving to it, or resting from it. If work makes us miserable, our lives are going to be miserable. If we flounder in our work, it will affect all that we do.

A successful person must be successful at work. In this chapter we will explore what the Wisdom writers have to say about work. And we will discover principles that will help us to be more successful in our work and careers.

Developing the Right Attitude

Work existed before the first couple disobeyed God and fell into sin. God created a beautiful garden and put Adam and Eve there "to cultivate it and keep it" (Genesis 2:15). The word *cultivate* may be literally translated "work." Right here at the beginning of God's revelation to humanity, we discover that work is intrinsically good. The words that are used in Genesis 2:15 are also used to refer to "service to God."[6] This suggests that our work is one way to *serve* God. This truth is reinforced by Paul who wrote to the Colossians saying, "Whatever you do, do your work heartily, as for the Lord rather than for men" (Colossians 3:23).

It is true that work became more difficult after humanity's fall into sin. Because of Adam's disobedience, God cursed the ground so that it would produce its fruit only through much effort. But work is not the result of the curse and should not be viewed negatively. Work is good. It is intrinsically good. Work is also good for what it produces and leads to. Work is a productive activity that can be done as service to the Lord and for the benefit of humanity.

King Solomon had a positive attitude toward work. He advised that we "enjoy" ourselves in all our labors (Ecclesiastes 5:18). Henry Giles (1809-82), an American theologian, wrote:

> Man must work. That is certain as the sun. But he may work grudgingly or he may work gratefully; he may work as a man, or he may work as a machine. There is no work so rude, that he may not exalt it; no work so impassive, that he may not breathe a

---

[6] R. Paul Stevens, *Work Matters: Lessons from Scripture* (Grand Rapids: William B. Eerdmans Publishing Company, 2012), p. 11.

soul into it; no work so dull that he may not enliven it.[7]

In pruning roses, we can wither focus on those nasty thorns or on the lovely rose buds that result from our effort. The difference is in our attitude.

Most people don't enjoy all kinds of work equally. I admit that I enjoy teaching more than cleaning bathrooms. But by God's grace, we can change our negative attitude about any job into a positive one. We can learn to enjoy a task that might otherwise be viewed as unpleasant.

When I began teaching, I dreaded grading papers and exams. It was time-consuming, mentally taxing, and seemed to offer few rewards. But realizing that grading is an inevitable part of teaching, I decided that a change of attitude was in order. I determined to make my grading a ministry of encouragement to my students. I began reading each paper for something worthy of commendation. Soon I realized that grading papers gave me a unique opportunity to relate to my students individually. Then I began to discover that students often have some pretty good things to say, so I started taking notes. Now I find that I actually enjoy grading! What was formerly an unpleasant task is now a challenging opportunity.

We can all experience such a change of attitude regarding our work by finding something meaningful or enjoyable in the task. We must recognize that work is the means to significant accomplishment. By focusing on the end result or the benefit to others, we can experience a more positive attitude toward our work.

Recognizing the Right Priorities

According to Solomon, the wise and successful person makes work a priority. "He who gathers in summer is a son who acts wisely, but he who sleeps in harvest is a son who acts shamefully" (Proverbs 10:5). This is another way of saying, "Make hay while the sun shines." A wise farmer will work hard during the summer harvest and rest when the

---

[7] *The New Dictionary of Thoughts*, p. 741

work is done. He knows that the opportunity to work is limited. Even the ants recognize this truth. "The ants are not strong folk, but they prepare their food in the summer" (Proverbs 30:25).

This is not to suggest that we must be "workaholics" in order to be successful. Excessive devotion to work is just as much an imbalance as excessive devotion to leisure. It is essential for us to balance work with rest. This is the basis for the biblical principle of Sabbath rest (Exodus 20:8-11). But if we want to be successful, we will make work a high priority in life. Work won't be neglected. We will get it done first.

When Charles M. Schwab, the American steel magnate, wrote his "Ten Commandments of Success," he put "hard work" at the very top of the list. "Hard work," he said, "is the best investment a man [or woman] can make."

For many years I heated part of my house with a wood stove. I spent many of my "days off" cutting and splitting firewood for winter. It was a chore that was easy for me to put off. I'd rather be hiking or fishing. But I discovered that I enjoyed my summer recreation more if I got my work done *first*. Once my wood cutting was finished, I could enjoy some Saturday hiking and fishing trips. And I enjoyed those recreational activities without a sense of uneasiness or guilt because my work was done.

Anyone can learn to make work a priority. I knew of a woman who hated to wash breakfast dishes, so she would pile them in the sink. All day she avoided the mess and felt a sense of guilt over neglecting this chore. At the suggestion of a friend, she decided to do the dishes the first thing after breakfast, and then take a coffee break to celebrate. She is a happier and more successful homemaker today because she made her work a priority.

Enjoying the Rewards of Work

Work pays dividends. It yields success. Thomas Edison denied that he was a genius in any sense of the word. He also refuted the suggestion that his success as an inventor was due to chance discovery. "I never did anything worth doing by accident," he said, "nor did any of my inventions come by accident." Edison attributed his success to one thing—dedicated work.

The eloquent American statesman, Alexander Hamilton, attested to the rewards of work:

> Men give me some credit for genius. All the genius I have lies just in this: When I have a subject in hand, I study it profoundly. Day and night it is before me. I explore it in all its bearings. My mind becomes pervaded with it. Then the effort which I made the people are pleased to call the fruit of genius. It is the fruit of labor and thought.

The Wisdom writers of the Hebrew Bible state quite clearly that work yields fruit. Solomon said, "He who tills his land will have plenty of food, but he who follows empty pursuits will have poverty in plenty" (Proverbs 28:19). In another place, he declared, "In all labor there is profit, but mere talk leads only to poverty" (Proverbs 14:23). There is a time to leave off with the talk and move on to the toil. The profit is in the performance of the task.

A side benefit of work was highlighted by Solomon in Ecclesiastes 5:12, "The sleep of the working man is pleasant, whether he eats little or much. But the full stomach of the rich man does not allow him to sleep." We are more apt to rest well when our minds and bodies have been vigorously exercised. One of the best cures for sleeplessness is a good day of hard work.

Hard work is therapeutic. Hard physical exercise helps clear one's mind of weighty burdens and concerns. Thomas Edison put it well when he quipped, "As a cure for worrying, work is better than whiskey!" Those whose occupations involve more mental activity than physical labor need a program of exercise for psychological as well as physical reasons.

But what happens when our work is not rewarded? We have all had work experiences where there was no financial return or expression of appreciation. The Apostle Paul gave us an encouraging word for such times. "Whatever you do, do your work heartily, as for the Lord rather than for men; knowing that from the Lord you will receive the reward of the inheritance. It is the Lord Christ whom you serve" (Colossians 3:23-24). God in heaven keeps the accounts. A worker may not receive all the pay he or she may deserve, but one-day God's books will be balanced and the reward for your work will be paid in full.

Developing Diligence in Work

In 1949 an unknown American scientist started research on poliomyelitis (polio virus) with hopes of developing an immunization against the crippling disease. He worked with diligence—sixteen to eighteen hours a day, six days a week, for five years. Not only did the polio vaccine save tens of thousands lives, Dr. Jonas Salk made medical history. His success was the reward for his diligence in work.

Israel's sages not only commend work; they encourage *diligence* in work. "The soul of the sluggard craves and gets nothing, buy the soul of the diligent is made fat" (Proverbs 13:4). "The plans of the diligent lead surely to advantage, but everyone who is hasty comes surely to poverty" (Proverbs 21:5). "Poor is he who works with a negligent hand, but the hand of the diligent makes rich" (Proverbs 10:4).

We can do a job without giving it our best. Solomon said that while it pays to work, *diligent* work pays higher dividends. The diligent worker will be recognized and trusted with greater tasks and more responsibility. "The hand of diligent will rule" (Proverbs 12:24). Diligence is the pathway to career advancement. Solomon was right, "The precious possession of a man is diligence" (Proverbs 12:27).

Diligence is great! But what if we just don't have it? Is there any hope for a sluggard? I believe that diligence can be cultivated and developed. *First*, no matter what the job, we can do it as unto the Lord (Ephesians 6:6-7). Do we work harder when the boss is watching? A Christian serves the Almighty God and He never ceases to observe the work of His people. We must do our best for Him—always.

Second, we must recognize that diligence pays high dividends, including having provisions, possessions, and prominence (Proverbs 13:4; 10:4; 12:24). *Third,* we must appreciate that failure to exercise diligence is costly. Lack of diligence may result in danger or poverty, or even cost a job promotion.

Successful workers go the extra mile. They put in additional effort and strive for excellence in their work. As Solomon said, "Whatever your hand finds to do, do it with all your might" (Ecclesiastes 9:10). Some people work less when they are paid a minimum wage. But they will never earn a raise by minimal performance. Folks who never do any more than they get paid for never get paid for any more than they do.

On a shelf in my office are two tempered steel rivets that serve to remind me of the dividends of diligence. The rivets attached my clutch fork to the bell housing on my 1969 Cougar. When they sheared, I was told that replacement would require dismantling the parking-brake cables, removing the drive shaft, and dropping the transmission—at a cost of about $1,000. Before spending that kind of money I decided to attempt the repair myself, without removing the bell housing.

I spent most of the day under my car tapping, drilling, and twisting those rivets. My muscles ached. Oily grime dropped into my eyes. I wanted to quit and pay a mechanic to do the repair. But I stuck with the job and gave it my extra effort. Finally, the rivets loosened and dropped into my hand. I replaced them with bolts and installed the clutch fork. It worked perfectly! My extra effort saved me a big repair bill and taught me an unforgettable lesson on the rewards of diligence.

Avoiding the Folly of Slothfulness
Benjamin Franklin once said, "Sloth, like rust, consumes faster than labor wears, while the key often used is always bright." Have you ever seen a sloth? If not, go on-line and find a video clip of a sloth crawling. Sloths move only when

necessary and even then, their slow movements give the impression that they are lazy. The Book of Proverbs uses the image of the sloth to describe a slow, sluggish, and lazy person. What does Proverbs tell us about the character of a slothful person?

The sluggard doesn't start things. "How long will you lie down, O sluggard? When will you arise from your sleep?" (Proverbs 6:9). The sluggard prefers rest to work (Proverbs 26:14). Instead of plowing the ground for planting, he procrastinates until it is too late (Proverbs 20:4). He substitutes wishing for work; lounging for labor.

The sluggard doesn't finish things. He is too lazy to cook the game he has caught and allows the meat to spoil (Proverbs 12:27). He begins to eat, but "buries his hand in the dish," too lazy to finish the meal that has been prepared (Proverbs 26:15).

The sluggard makes excuses for his laziness. "There is a lion outside," he says, "I shall be slain in the streets" (Proverbs 22:13). The sluggard always has reasonably sounding excuses for his lack of discipline and refusal to work.

The sluggard can't be taught. "The sluggard is wiser in his own eyes than seven men who give a discreet answer" (Proverbs 26:16). He considers himself more competent than those who have had more training. The sluggard is not likely to take advice or learn from others.

What fate awaits the sluggard? Solomon tells of his destiny. The sluggard will face severe poverty (Proverbs 6:11; 24:34), suffer hunger (19:15), and have to beg for food (20:4). He will be ruled by his constant but unsatisfied desires (21:26). His path of life will be difficult—like a road obstructed by a vast hedge of thorns (15:19). His ultimate fate is ruin and death (21:25).

Not everyone who lives on the streets and holds up a sign asking for money from strangers is a sluggard. Many have legitimate physical and mental needs. But some may match the description of a sluggard. I recall a radio interview with a street person who described his homeless situation as a "lifestyle choice." He had a good job in the past, but gave it up. He explained that he liked the freedom to be able to come and go as he pleased with no responsibilities or demands on his time. When he was asked whether he felt somewhat guilty living off the generosity of others who provided food and financial help, his answer was "Not at all! It is a great deal for me!" This seems to be the attitude of the sluggard.

Being a sluggard is not fun—it is folly. A premature retirement from the responsibilities of work is like a desert mirage. It looks so refreshing in the distance, but the pleasures promised dissipate in the face of life's realities.

Maintaining Honesty in Work

"Make yourself an honest man," Thomas Carlyle, the nineteenth-century English essayist, once quipped, "and then you may be sure there is one less rascal in the world."

Most of us want to be honest in what we say, but are we always honest in what we do? Do salesmen represent their products honestly? Is the price in keeping with the quality of the merchandise? Do workers give a full hour's work for an hour's pay? A ten minute breaks stretched to fifteen? Does Proverbs have anything to say about honesty in these matters?

God's concern for honesty in business is highlighted by Solomon's words concerning proper weights and balances. "A false balance is an abomination to the LORD, but a just weight is His delight" (Proverbs 11:1). When it comes to weighing or measuring merchandise, God is concerned that the buyer not be cheated. For the butcher to weigh his thumb on the scales with the meat is not only dishonest—it is repugnant to God. God likes a fair deal.

According to Solomon, those who profit illicitly are headed for trouble (Proverbs 16:27). While they might have some immediate satisfaction in "making an easy buck," they are destined for ultimate disappointment. "Bread obtained by falsehood is sweet to a man, but afterward his mouth will be filled with gravel" (20:17). In the end, the cheater pays for what he or she gets.

The guiding principle for honesty in work is found in Proverbs 28:16, "Better is the poor who walks in his integrity, than he who is crooked though he be rich." Solomon wasn't suggesting that we will be poor if we are honest in work and business. He was saying that it is *better* to be poor and have our integrity than to be rich crooks. A clear conscience and a good reputation cannot be bought at any price (Proverbs 22:1).

Learning to Work

The ability to work hard and achieve excellence is not a spiritual gift bestowed on a select few. Any willing person can become a diligent, successful worker. The following principles have been helpful to me in my career. Perhaps you can add to the list.

Learn from others. Solomon said, "Go to the ant, O sluggard, observe her ways and be wise" (Proverbs 6:6). I have found it helpful to observe the lives of other men and women who have been successful in their fields. I watch how they work and learn from their example. I learned a great deal about work from my own hard working Dad. We can learn much from those who have a successful track record.

Set priorities. Proverbs points out the difficulty of trying to rear a family when you have no shelter or means of financial support (24:27). We must first build a house, plant a vineyard, and then take a wife. It has been helpful for me to make a priority list of the things I need to do. I number the items on the list based on their importance or urgency. As I finish a task, I scratch it off the list and move on to the next thing on my "to do" list. No time is wasted fretting over what to do next. What a relief to scratch off the last item and throw the list away! My oldest son was recently home for a visit. I noticed that he had on his computer a list of the things he wanted to accomplish during the next month. I wonder where he got that idea?

Reward your diligent efforts. Solomon said, "A worker's appetite works for him, for his hunger urges him on" (Proverbs 16:26). If hunger will motivate someone to work, couldn't the anticipation of a break, an evening out, or a vacation function in a similar manner? I have sometimes rewarded myself with a Saturday morning fishing trip after completing a project. You could reward yourself with a refreshing lunch break after a busy morning's work. Even a small reward can be motivating. After washing the dishes after the evening meal, I often reward myself with a visit to the cookie jar. Sometimes after several hours of grading papers, I take a break and reward myself with a neighborhood walk. It has been helpful and motivating for me to set goals in my work and then reward myself when I accomplish my task. Working with a view to a reward may be helpful for you as well.

Divide big jobs into small tasks. Sometimes when we look at a job that needs to be done, we feel overwhelmed by the enormity of the project. When I was in my doctoral program I wondered how I could write a three to four-hundred-page dissertation? Where should I begin? When I was able to catch my breath in the face of this huge project, I divided it into small parts that I knew I could accomplish. I divided the dissertation into chapters and the chapters into sections. I knew that I could write a couple of pages on each section. I set as my goal writing a few pages a day, a section each week, and a chapter each month until the project was completed. Dividing big projects into smaller units was a key to completing my doctoral dissertation and has been a major factor in my successful accomplishment of many projects ever since.

Wise parents will teach their children at an early age to appreciate and enjoy work. I am thankful that my parents made work enjoyable. After working all Saturday in the garden with my dad, we would take a load of brush and clippings to the county dump. On the old dump road south of town dad would let me drive. Even before I had a learners permit, I would sit on my Dad's lap and he would operate the pedals while I steered the car. When we arrived back in town, Dad would treat me to a cold, foamy root beer at the A & W drive-in. By being paid for doing extra jobs around the house, I learned at an early age that money doesn't "grow on trees." I learned to value what work can do in bringing reward, satisfaction, and fulfillment.

I remember well spending a hard day of wood-cutting with my young son, John. On the drive home towing a trailer full of wood, he commented, "Dad, working is fun." What a privilege to be passing on to the next generation an appreciation for the value and reward of work. Viewing work with a positive attitude is another essential factor in living life successfully.

Study and Review Questions

1. Is work a part of the curse that resulted from Adam's fall? How might an incorrect understanding of the origin of work affect one's attitude toward it?
2. Is it possible to change one's attitude toward work? Suggest some creative ways to change an attitude toward an unpleasant job.
3. Why is it important to make work a priority? How does making work a priority better enable someone to enjoy recreation and leisure time?
4. According to the Wisdom Books, work pays dividends. What are the rewards of work that you have experienced and appreciate?
5. How can someone become a more diligent worker? What guidelines can you suggest?
6. According to Solomon, what is the destiny of those who refuse to work? Did the Apostle Paul have anything to say about this (2 Thessalonians 3:10)? Can you think of any legitimate reasons for someone not working?

7. What biblical evidence is there that God is interested in business ethics? How might your business or work situation be brought into greater conformity with God's standard?

Chapter 6
MANAGING YOUR MONEY

A wealthy businessman was asked the secret of his financial success. The millionaire responded, "I can attribute my success to a pattern consisting of four D's—dedication, determination, discipline, and the death of an uncle who left me $999,000."

Only a few are blessed with that kind of "success." Most of us must work hard to earn a living and provide for our families. We have to manage our money carefully to meet our obligations and avoid financial disaster. Yet in spite of our best efforts, many of God's people still struggle financially.

Well do I remember the financial difficulties I encountered shortly after my marriage! I was a seminary student and my new wife had just taken a job as a second-grade teacher. We expected to be able to live on her salary while I finished my studies.

Getting settled into an apartment was a bit more costly than we had expected. We bought a sofa, a bed, and a few used chairs. It was a modest beginning, but considerably depleted our savings. Yet there was no need to worry. Nancy's monthly paychecks would soon provide for our ongoing needs.

With Nancy's first check we paid the rent and other bills, filled our car with gas, and bought groceries. During the third week of the month I was surprised to find our money nearly gone. This "more-month-at-the-end-of-the-money" syndrome was repeated the next month—and the next. I began to seriously suspect that we were being robbed! Our money was simply disappearing into thin air.

We managed to head off financial disaster by moving into a less expensive apartment and cutting expenses. As things settled down, I began to search the Scriptures for biblical principles that would help us to be good stewards of our resources and avoid future financial difficulties.

My quest took me to the writings of Solomon—the wealthiest ruler of ancient Israel. Solomon's prosperity wasn't an accident. He knew the secret of financial success. In Proverbs, Solomon shared the key concepts that proved effected in enabling him to accumulate and manage a great deal of wealth. Exploring these principles will help us gain a biblical perspective on money and teach us how to use it more wisely. There is no guarantee that we will become as wealthy as Solomon. But we can avoid economic chaos and gain financial freedom by applying the time-proven principles of Israel's most successful businessman.

Gaining Perspective on Wealth

George H. Lorimer, former editor of *The Saturday Evening Post*, had a proper perspective on wealth. "It's good to have money, and the things money can buy; but it's good, too, to check up once in a while and make sure that you haven't lost the things that money *can't* buy."

Jay Gould was a multimillionaire, but he wasn't happy. On his deathbed, he said, "I suppose I am the most miserable man on earth." Money can't buy a happy marriage, obedient children, or enjoyment in one's work. Gordon P. Getty, one of the richest men in America, concurs. "The best things in life require effort and study rather than money."

Solomon said that wisdom was more important than wealth. "How blessed is the man who finds wisdom, and the man who gains understanding. For its profit is better than the profit of silver, and its gain than fine gold. She is more precious than jewels; and nothing you desire compares with her" (Proverbs 3:13-15). Wisdom, integrity, and a good reputation, concluded Solomon, are of far greater value than riches (19:1; 22:1).

Tapping his unlimited financial resources, Solomon conducted an experiment to see if the things money can buy would bring lasting satisfaction (Ecclesiastes 2:4-8). He built houses, planted vineyards, made gardens, parks, and ponds. He bought servants, flocks, and herds. He acquired great treasure. What was the outcome of Solomon's experiment? He concluded, "Thus I considered

concept of being a cosigner. The cosigner assumes legal responsibility for the payment of the debt should the borrower default. Solomon warned against such financial entanglements and counsels those so encumbered to deliver themselves (Proverbs 6:1-5). He wrote, "He who is surety for a stranger will surely suffer for it, but he who hates going surety is safe" (11:15).

Solomon was not suggesting that we become callous to the needs of others. Rather, he was warning against "losing our shirt" through the mismanagement of our money by others. Solomon explained, "If you have nothing with which to pay, why should he take your bed from under you?" (22:27). A harsh creditor might require you to give up some essential property in order to pay the debt you have assumed.

A wise person will beware of a relationship or agreement that makes him or her legally responsible for the debts incurred by the partner. Before becoming a cosigner for a friend or relative, it would be wise to consider the following questions: (1) Is the purchase really necessary? (2) In case of default, can I pay the obligation without endangering my own financial well-being or peace of mind? (3) What effect will this commitment have on my relationship with the one for whom I am cosigner.

The more common financial entanglement for Americans today is debt. You don't have to be a financial wizard to see that living on credit is getting millions of people into financial trouble. The accumulation of personal debt in America is staggering. Recent figures indicate that the average American family owes $7,950 in credit card debt, $11,244 in student loans, $8,163 on their automobiles, and $70,322 on their mortgages. According to 2015 figures, student loan debt has reached 1.2 trillion dollars and $66.7 billion is being carried by borrowers over sixty years old.[10] A growing number of older Americans will carry student debt into retirement. We are a nation that is living on money that we have not yet earned. And that is a

---

[10] *Time* (February 20, 2017), p. 22.

dangerous situation for our nation and ourselves individually.

More frequently than ever before, Americans are finding that they can't pay their debts. There were 911,086 personal bankruptcies filed in 2015. Perhaps you can identify with a couple I read about who both work and together earn $80,000 a year. They live with their eight-year-old son in a modest, renovated home in a nice neighborhood. They have a new car and a new kitchen. There is just one problem. They are broke! And they are deeply in debt. "The question is," says the working wife and mother, "shall we eat this week or pay the electric bill?"

The specter of debt! Solomon recognized its hidden hazards and warned of the bondage it brings. "The rich rules over the poor and the borrower becomes the lender's slave" (Proverbs 22:7). Charles Spurgeon warned his parishioners, "Poverty is hard, but debt is horrible. A man might as well have a smoky house and a scolding wife."

Ben Franklin said that running into debt would give others "power over your liberty." He added, "If you cannot pay at the time, you will be ashamed to see your creditor; will be in fear when you speak to him; will make poor, pitiful, sneaking excuses, and by degrees come to lose your veracity, and sink into base, downright lying; for the second vice is lying, the first is running into debt."

Is it possible to avoid going into debt? I believe it is. The following guidelines will enable you to guard yourself against the plunge into debt.

Don't spend what you don't have. This simple principle led me out of the financial chaos I experienced early in my marriage. When I realized that we were spending more money than Nancy was making as a second grade teacher, we cut expenses and established a budget to regulate our spending. Finance companies tempt us, "Enjoy your family vacation now! You can pay us back later!" But borrowing now will cost more later—in interest, anxiety, and trouble. Borrowing a "little" may lead to borrowing a lot. This pattern will lead to financial disaster.

Pay cash for your purchases. It is amazing to see the difference between the cash and credit price. I noticed automobile dealers feature in their advertising the monthly payments rather than the price of the car. People seem to be more interested in how much they can pay monthly rather than the total price of the vehicle. When you add interest payments on $30,000 over five years, you add several thousand dollars to the price of the car. That may not seem like a lot, but it would pay for a nice vacation or be a good start on a retirement "nest egg." The alternative for the credit-conscious person may be to purchase a good quality used car and pay cash. Paying with cash is a continual reminder of the true cost of my purchases. And it is a visual lesson for my observant children that nothing in life but our salvation is really free.

Destroy your credit cards. It sounds pretty extreme, doesn't it? Yet for the undisciplined, credit spending is dangerous. Some debt ridden Americans have whole collection of credit cards and carry debt on each one. They have to get new loans just to meet the monthly minimum payments due on one account or another.

Now if you are careful and disciplined, credit cards can be helpful when paying for things like airline tickets and items purchased on the internet. The key is to avoid the 21 percent interest charge by paying the bill in full at the end of the month. You may be able to take advantage of a sale by using a credit card. For disciplined spenders, it is helpful to retain and use one major credit card. But beware of the danger of cumulative debt.

Avoid spur-of-the-moment purchases. When shopping, it is good to have a list of those items you really need. Make the purchases you planned and then head for home! A new tool or fishing rod may catch my attention. I want it! The price tag says, "Buy me now!" I could probably afford the purchase, but is it something I really need? The fact is, I didn't know I wanted it until I saw it at the store!

I've made it a general policy to go home and think over such a purchase. Just getting out of the store without the item has saved me lots of money. Later I might return for the purchase if I decide that the purchase is really necessary. But frequently I decide that the item is something I can get along just as well without. There were many times I walked into the tire shop, admired the shiny chrome wheels, and pondered how they would look on my van. But so far, I have managed to get home with my planned purchase of new tires and without a set of expensive chrome wheels.

Avoid borrowing money on depreciating items. Many of the things we buy on credit depreciate. They decline in value from use. This is true of automobiles, appliances, and clothes. If we encounter financial difficulties, we would not be able to sell the item for its original price and pay the debt. The purchase of a home is a different matter. It seems reasonable to take a mortgage for such a purchase. Few of us could pay cash for a home. And homes generally appreciate in value, although not always. Many people who bought new homes at the peak of the housing market found themselves "under water" when the housing market crashed in 2008. Borrowing money always has risks, and this is especially true on depreciating items.

Prepare a budget to help with financial planning. A budget frees the careful planner to buy those items in the budget. Having money budgeted for entertainment means that I can take my wife out for the evening without the uneasy feeling that the money should have gone for groceries. My family budget includes charitable and church giving, house payments, food, clothes, medical expenses, transportation, utilities, savings and miscellaneous. If my anticipated expenses exceed my income, something has to be cut. I may have to cut my entertainment or start taking the bus to work. But to go on spending what I don't have is unthinkable. That is not the way to financial success.

Investing Money Wisely

Someone with an income of $3,000 per month will have $1,440,000 pass through his or her hands during the earning years from age 25 to 65. How much of that money will that person have at retirement? Probably none of it, unless they know the secret of monetary accumulation. This secret is known to every successful investor. I learned the secret from a well-known financial advisor of the 1980s.[11] The secret is so simple that people may be tempted to ignore it. But if it is applied to financial affairs, it will enable someone to be financially successful, making adequate preparation for the needs of the future.

The secret is this: A part of all you earn is yours to keep. Now you might be thinking, *everything* I earn is mine to keep. But remember that part of your monthly check goes to the mortgage company, part to the IRS, part to your place of worship, and part to the grocer. Trying to keep some leftover money for savings is just about impossible these days. It takes planning and discipline. But to be successful financially, you *must* pay yourself along with your other obligations.

Scripture encourages wise stewardship of one's financial resources (Matthew 25:14-30). Solomon himself commended the one whose wise financial dealings enabled him to acquire an estate for his heirs. "A good man leaves an inheritance to his children's children" (Proverbs 13:22). Careful financial planning and investing requires work and study, but the ultimate rewards far outweigh the initial effort involved (Proverbs 14:4).

Solomon offered some helpful suggestions for those who wish to invest their savings wisely. First, a wise investor recognizes the inherent risk involved and guards against financial disaster. Solomon wrote, "When those

---

[11] Venita VanCaspel, Money Dynamics for the 1980s (Reston, Va.: Reston Publishing Co., Inc. 1980).

81

riches were lost through a bad investment and he had fathered a son, then there is nothing to support him" (Ecclesiastes 5:14). Most investors will lose some money due to the inherent risk of investing. Even a savings account involves a risk—the risk of losing the purchasing power of your money due to inflation. Solomon advised the investor to avoid risking what he or she cannot afford to lose.

Generally speaking, higher risk investments have a higher potential for gain. But if you are not too excited about the possibility of losing money on an investment, perhaps you should consider more conservative opportunities such as index funds, bonds, and certificates of deposit.

Investors ought not to turn up their noses at a guaranteed interest rate that offers a lower rate of return than a more speculative investment. If you were to invest $100 per month for thirty years at with 8% annual rate of a rate of return, you would have a nest egg of $186,253.14. While this is not enough to retire on, it is a good example of how a regular savings and investment plan can build your estate. And if you can save $100 per month at age 30, you may be able to save $200 per month at age forty. And the more you save, the more your estate will grow to provide a resource for your future retirement needs. Forty years ago I started saving $50.00 per month. Over the years I have added to my savings program, raising my monthly contribution again, again, again. I did this because early in my career I learned the secret to financial success: "A part of all you earn is yours to keep."

Solomon offered a second important investment principle: "Divide your portion into seven, or even to eight, for you do not know what misfortune may occur on the earth" (Ecclesiastes 11:2). There is great wisdom in diversifying your investments. This is simply making a practical application of the proverb, "Don't put all your eggs in one basket." If your investments are diversified, you won't suffer as great a loss should one of them go sour. My investments include stocks, bonds, a savings account, and real property (my home). Some of these investments have done better than others. My best investment so far has been my home.

Here is another tip in the area of investing: Get professional help. Expert counsel in the area of financial planning and investing is well worth the commission paid on the investments. Mutual funds (in which resources are pooled with other investors) not only provide diversification but also professional management of the resources. A full-time management team does market research, selects the best investments, and constantly supervises the fund's portfolio. These full-time professionals will better enable a person to invest his or her money wisely.

Giving to God and Those in Need

Far from being a burden, the wise person views giving as a blessed opportunity. Solomon said, "Happy is he who is gracious to the poor" (Proverbs 14:21). He declared, "He who is generous will be blessed, for he gives some of his food to the poor" (22:9). I am learning to appreciate what money can do for others. That appreciation is freeing me from the bondage of addiction to miserly accumulation of money. There is great joy that comes from investing in God's kingdom work and sharing with those in need.

In the area of giving, there is a biblical priority. Solomon said, "Honor the LORD from your wealth, and from the first of all your produce; so your barns will be filled with plenty, and your vats will overflow with new wine" (Proverbs 3:9-10). God is honored when we give Him the *first* of our income, not the "leftovers" (1 Corinthians 16:2; Mark 12:44).

When we plan our budgets, we should decide what we want to give the Lord. Then we should write the Lord's check first, and trust God to meet our other needs and obligations. According to Scripture, He will provide abundantly. "And my God will supply all your needs according to His riches in glory in Christ Jesus" (Philippians 4:19). "And God is able to make all grace abound to you, so that always having all sufficiency in everything, you may have an abundance for every good deed" (2 Corinthians 9:8).

Solomon also commended the one who is generous to the poor and needy (Proverbs 21:13; 11:25). According to Solomon, "He who gives to the poor will never want" (28:27). Being gracious to the poor actually honors God (14:31). What we lend or give the poor may never be returned directly, but Solomon assures us, "He who is gracious to a poor man lends to the Lord, and He will repay him for his good deed" (19:17).

Over the years I have wrestled with how to respond to people standing on the street corner or freeway entrance with a sign, "Anything helps. God bless." The people have obvious needs. What is the best way to help alleviate their situation? A cash gift may make me feel better, but I don't know if the money will go for food, cigarettes or drugs. I have decided that the best way to help the homeless and those in need is to contribute to a local mission that specializes in helping those who are destitute and living on the streets. Portland Rescue Mission is one such organization which provides food, shelter, and clothing to needy people. I have confidence that the money I give to this ministry will be used wisely and well.

What do you do when a friend or relative asks for a loan? My experience in lending to those in need has been that a debtor-creditor relationship frequently diminishes and sometimes destroys the friendship between two people. It may be better to give money than to loan it. If someone wants to borrow $100, we might say, "I can't lend you $100, but I can give you $50 as a gift." This practice has enabled me to avoid negative feelings toward those who might delay paying back a loan or fail to pay it altogether.

Possessing, or Being Possessed

Tyrone Edwards, great-grandson of the famed Jonathan Edwards, had a biblical perspective on money. He wrote, "To possess money is very well; it may be a most valuable servant; to be possessed by it, is to be possessed by a devil, and one of the meanest and worst kinds of devils." Money is a good servant, but a poor master. Those who aspire to be successful will maintain this biblical perspective as they exercise stewardship over their financial resources.

I have found that being generous toward my church and other charitable organizations frees me from being possessed by my financial resources. And there is great joy and satisfaction that comes from investing in ministries that help people both physically and spiritually. These are investments that count for eternity.

When it comes to giving, I recommend the practice of "open handed generosity." Someone has said, "You can't out give God." My giving is simply an acknowledgment of the fact that I am a steward of what God has entrusted to me. Some of what God has entrusted to my care will be used for my needs and the needs of my family. But some of my financial resources have been entrusted to me to share.

Being a successful person doesn't mean having lots of money. It does mean that we know how to use the money we do have wisely and well. Godly stewardship of resources rather than the accumulation of wealth is the *biblical* measure of financial success.

Study and Review Questions

1. On a scale of one to ten (one poor, ten perfect), rate your "financial quotient." Consider these areas: perspective on wealth, avoidance of debt, investment strategy, and giving. Recognizing your areas of need is the first step toward financial stability. Where do you need the most help?
2. Summarize in your own words a biblical perspective on wealth. What part should contentment play in your attitude toward money?
3. What are the proper means of gaining wealth? What methods should you as a Christian avoid?
4. What financial entanglements presently have their hold on you? Of the six guidelines for avoiding

financial entanglements, which need application in your own life?

5. Do you have a budget? If not, prepare one now. If you already have a budget, take time to review it. Does it accurately represent your needs and guide your spending?

6. Do you have a systematic plan for saving a part of your income for future needs? What principles should guide a wise investment program?

7. What biblical principles should direct your giving? What place does giving to those in need have in your giving plans?

Chapter 7
BUILDING A LASTING MARRIAGE

I was just ten years old when I decided that, as a confirmed bachelor, I needed to learn to cook. I practiced on Saturday mornings making breakfast for the rest of my family. My two specialties were pancakes and oatmeal. But since those items were rather ordinary, I sought to liven them up a bit. I accomplished my objective by adding food coloring. You can imagine the look on my dad's face the morning I served him up a bowl full of hot, steaming, green oatmeal!

One day I decided I was ready for a more advanced recipe. I determined to make a Jell-O salad. I knew that the key to making Jell-O was to use a gelatin mold. Finding one in my mother's cupboard, I mixed, instead of Jell-O, a package of lime Kool-Aid. Not having any fruit on hand to mix with it, I decided that several sticks of chewing gum would give it that "extra something."

The dinner hour arrived, but my "Jell-O" wasn't ready. The next day it still hadn't firmed up. Finally, my mother took me aside and explained to me the sober reality that my Kool-Aid would never become Jell-O. Undaunted, I drank the Kool-Aid and chewed the gum.

My attempt to make Jell-O failed because I didn't have the proper ingredients. You must have the right ingredients to make a tasty Jell-O salad. The same is true of marriage.

All of us are rightly concerned about the divorce epidemic that is shattering homes and families throughout America. Research indicates that up to fifty percent of marriages end in divorce. And the divorce rate is even higher for second marriages. More frequently than ever before, we hear of Christian leaders whose marriages have failed.

Most people work hard to make their marriages meaningful and lasting. They want a marriage that is happy and joyful with a minimum of conflict, pain, and struggle. Yet many marriages fail to meet these expectations. Often the reason can be traced to the fact that the couple overlooked several essential ingredients. The Word of God provides us with a recipe—ten essential ingredients for a successful and lasting marriage.

Total Commitment

Total commitment to the marriage and to each other is essential for a lasting marriage. This ingredient is reflected in the "cleaving" mentioned in God's description of marriage. God said, "For this cause a man shall leave his father and his mother, and shall cleave to his wife; and they shall become one flesh" (Genesis 2:24).

Many people enter marriage today with the viewpoint that if it doesn't work, they can get a divorce and try again. This attitude is like tolerating a crack in the Hoover Dam. Sooner or later the irritating circumstances common to all marriages, like water leaking through the crack, will erode away enough material to precipitate a collapse.

Commitment to marriage involves a recognition that marriage is more than just a legal agreement. The Bible calls it a "covenant" (Proverbs 2:17; Malachi 2:14). Marriage involves a vow or promise that makes the obligation binding (Numbers 30:2). The significance of a promise is highlighted in the words of a former seminary professor, Lewis Smedes: "When you make a promise you have created a small sanctuary of trust within the jungle of unpredictability. Human destiny rests on a promise freely given and reliably remembered."[12]

Commitment to marriage involves a recognition that marriage was designed by God to be permanent until death.[13] The Jewish leaders asked Jesus where He stood on the controversial issue of divorce. He responded, "What therefore God has joined together, let no man separate" (Matthew 19:6).

---

[12] Lewis B. Smedes, "The Power of Promising," *Christianity Today*, January 21, 1983, p. 17.

[13] For a detailed study of God's plan for the permanence of marriage, see my book, *The Divorce Myth* (Minneapolis: Bethany House Publishers, 1981).

The Pharisees countered, "But didn't Moses allow divorce?" Jesus explained that Moses permitted divorce because of the Israelites' hard hearts. Then He added, "But from the beginning it has not been this way" (19:8). God's original plan was that marriage be a lifelong relationship.

The launch of a space rocket or vehicle involves a long countdown, which gives the ground crew time to check and recheck all the operating systems. The launch can be delayed at any point in the countdown before ignition. But when lift-off takes place, there must be a total commitment to the launch. Once the craft is fifty feet off the pad, there is no way to bring it back down safely. So it is with marriage. When you say, "I do," there must be a total commitment to the marriage for life.

Total commitment involves love that gives and gives for the benefit of the other person. Paul said, "Husbands, love your wives, just as Christ also loved the church" (Ephesians 5:25). The same applies to wives (5:22). How did Christ love the church?" He gave Himself up for her. He totally abandoned Himself for the ultimate good of the church.

Marriage is not a fifty-fifty arrangement. It takes total commitment on the part of both partners to build a successful and lasting marriage.

Total Acceptance

In marriage we should accept our partner as he or she is. Many couples spend their lives nagging each other about personal habits and idiosyncrasies they have no power to change. Paul addressed this matter when he wrote: "Wherefore, accept one another, just as Christ also accepted us to the glory of God" (Romans 15:7).

Most of us have had more than a few surprises during our first year of marriage. What husband or wife ever lived up to all those romantic expectations? But nagging will never change our partners much. It will only irritate them and make us bitter.

If we have a major problem with our spouse, we should make it a matter of prayer. Perhaps the Lord will change *us!* We must learn to appreciate the peculiarities of our spouse as evidences of the unique and special individual God has made that person.

Loving Communication

I believe in honest communication. I like to "tell it like it is." But I've discovered that the hard, cold facts can be hurtful. Instead of bringing healing and harmony, blunt and brutal truth can harm a relationship. Solomon warns us of the dangers of a thoughtless word, "There is one who speaks rashly like the thrusts of a sword" (Proverbs 12:18). Paul provided the key to successful communication: "But speaking the truth in love, we are to grow up in all aspects into Him" (Ephesians 4:15).

Every couple needs to set aside time to talk about plans, problems, grievances, or misunderstandings. In discussing these matters, they should focus on the problem and avoid attacking the other person.

An old sheepherder saw a pack of wolves attack a band of wild ponies. The ponies formed a circle with their heads in the center and kicked at the wolves, driving them away. Later he witnessed a band of wild donkeys being attacked by wolves. They too formed a circle, but faced the wolves. When the wolves attacked, they kicked *each other* instead of the foe. Loving communication lets the truth be known, but it does so in such a way as to edify the partner and build up the marriage.

Genuine Forgiveness

Someone has said that the only perfect people are bachelors' wives and old maids' children. The fact is, nobody's perfect. And that state of affairs demands a lot of genuine forgiveness in marriage.

Peter asked the Lord, "How often shall my brother sin against me and I forgive him? Up to seven times?" (Matthew 18:21). The rabbis said three times was enough. Peter doubled it and added one for good measure. But

Jesus challenged this sort of thinking that places a limitation on forgiveness.

"I do not say to you, up to seven times, but up to seventy times seven" (Matthew 18:22). In other words, if you are still counting, you are not exercising genuine forgiveness. Jesus went on to tell the parable of the unforgiving slave (18:23-35). The lesson is clear. In view of the infinite debt forgiven us, we have no right to refuse forgiveness to others. "If you do not forgive men, then your Father will not forgive your transgressions" (Matthew 6:15).

I learned a lesson in forgiveness during my college days, when I received permission from my dad to take his car on a weekend outing. In preparing the car for the trip, I had it parked in our steep driveway. Apparently, I did not set the parking brake firmly. I went inside to get something and when I returned, the car had rolled out of the driveway and crashed into a brick wall across the street. The accident banged up the bumper and grill and put the car out of commission. It appeared that my weekend plans were ruined.

When dad came home that evening, I explained what happened. I was surprised—but gratified—with his response. "Accidents can happen," he said. "You can take my other car on your trip."

Someone may be thinking, "Well, anybody can forgive a dented fender. How about something as awful as adultery?" God gives us the answer to that issue too. Hosea's adulterous wife, Gomer, actually became a temple prostitute. Yet God instructed Hosea, "Go again, love a woman who is loved by her husband, yet an adulteress" (Hosea 3:1). I am sure that it wasn't easy, but Hosea sought out his unfaithful wife and restored her to himself and to God. While this sin cannot be taken lightly (Proverbs 6:32-33), the example of Hosea reveals that forgiveness, rather than divorce, is God's method of dealing with marital infidelity.

Genuine forgiveness of even the worst sin is not only essential to a successful marriage; it is essential to the

enjoyment of God's blessing. God will not bless an
unforgiving heart.

Role Relationships

Many people today would like to convince us that there are
no differences between men and women. But there is little
biblical support for this viewpoint, which would totally do
away with role relationships for husbands and wives. Paul
said, "The husband is the head of the wife, as Christ also is
the head of the church" (Ephesians 5:23). God has a
design for order and authority in the home. A successful
marriage will function according to His design, not contrary
to it.

Much of the confusion on this issue is due to the false
assumption that if a woman's role is different from a man's,
she must be inferior. But nowhere in the Bible is there
anything to support this view. Christ has a role that is
different from the Father, yet they are equal in their divinity,
authority, and power (John 5:19-29; Corinthians 11:3).

According to Peter, a woman is equal to a man in
spiritual privilege as "a fellow-heir of the grace of life" (1
Peter 3:7). Yet God directed wives to submit themselves to
their husbands (3:1). The Bible clearly reveals that order
and authority are not incompatible with spiritual equality.

According to Scripture, there are two main roles for
spouses in marriage. The husband's role is that of a
"sacrificial lover" (Ephesians 5:25). Husbands are to love
their wives as Christ loved the church—to the point of
personal sacrifice. The wife's role is that of a "submissive
helper" (5:22, Genesis 2:18). The word "submissive" does
not suggest that she has no say in family decisions. She is
a valuable contributor of information and wisdom that
forms the basis of those decisions. And when a tough
decision must be made, she is willing and ready to support
the leadership of her husband.

The husband has authority in the home, but he is not a
dictator. Nor is the wife to be a doormat. The husband is to
exercise his leadership with genuine love, spiritual wisdom,

and personal sacrifice. The wife is to exercise her submission with assistance, support, and respect.

Spiritual Kinship

For a strong and successful marriage, a Christian husband and wife must develop a spiritual kinship—a sense of being co-laborers for Christ with a joint mission in life. Spiritual kinship is not something we get by reading a book or hearing a sermon. It is the result of prayer, sharing, sacrifice, study, and hard work, as a team effort. It is the result of developing a ministry together.

My duties at seminary and as a pastor require a lot of hospitality. During a single week my wife, Nancy, and I opened our home on four different evenings, entertaining a total of fifty-three people. It was lots of hard work. But as we shared in the ministry of setup and cleanup together, we had a greater sense of being co-laborers for Christ. Our spiritual kinship was strengthened as a result.

Spouses need to share in each other's lives and ministries. Praying together, working together, and dreaming together will help build a spiritual kinship and a lasting marriage.

Growing Friendship

The friendship of David and Jonathan was forged in the crucible of adversity. It was a friendship challenged by King Saul himself. Yet we read, "The soul of Jonathan was knit to the soul of David" (1 Samuel 18:1).

Is your spouse your best friend? Could you say that your soul is knit to the soul of your husband or wife? A growing friendship can be developed between husbands and wives. But it means they do for each other what friends do.

Friends do things together. They travel together, dine out together, shop together. I love taking my wife Nancy on a hike or a back packing trip. She enjoys it when I join her on a Sunday afternoon walk or bike ride. I seem to enjoy activities more when I am sharing them with my best friend. The activities we do together create a shared bank of memories we can draw upon for conversation and reflection. I love to think back and talk about the memories we have created over our forty-five years of marriage.

Flaming Romance

The Bible is quite forthright about developing the wholesomeness of sex in the marriage relationship (Proverbs 5:18-20). As we will discuss in the next chapter, sex was God's idea from the beginning. The physical expression of love in the marriage union must be viewed as a natural, healthy, and wholesome gift of God.

But in the rush of twenty-first century life, it is easy to neglect this most intimate and beautiful aspect of marriage. Hectic activity and late night television may be the biggest culprits. Neglect of the physical relationship in marriage results in a sense of isolation and loss of warmth and intimacy.

My advice is: turn off the tube. Take time for the marriage bed. Spend a weekend together at a resort hideaway. Study the Song of Solomon with your spouse. These special times are vital to the maintenance of a healthy romance with your spouse. They help keep couples focused on the *one* person God has given them to be intimate with and enables them to better steer clear of sexual temptation and compromise.

Good Humor

Someone has said, "There is no defense against adverse fortune so effectual as a good sense of humor." Solomon declared, "A joyful heart is good medicine" (Proverbs 17:22).

I make mistakes. I recently made a lot of them. I started off the day by oversleeping. Then my car wouldn't start. My morning lecture seemed as dry as dust. Then, when I arrived on campus for my evening class, I discovered I had forgotten my teaching notes. I could have gotten frustrated and angry, but that wouldn't have helped. Instead, I stepped into the men's room, looked in the mirror, and laughed at myself. It was as therapeutic as a good cry. I was able to relax and commit the evening to the Lord. In addition, I was able to remember most of the lecture material and had an enjoyable time of interaction with my students. A good sense of humor made the difference.

Married couples make mistakes. When they do, they can either laugh together or cry together. Certainly there is a time for both. But when as a couple they can laugh at errors in judgment, financial hardships, and personal trials, they are well on the road to a lasting marriage. Nothing helps more in dealing with turmoil, frustration, and conflict in marriage than having a good sense of humor.

Spiritual Rebirth

The most important ingredient to a lasting marriage is to have Jesus at the center of the marriage relationship. He will give strength, direction, balance, and stability to marriage and family life. This truth has been illustrated by a study done at the University of Virginia. Based on a nationwide survey, researchers concluded that couples who consider themselves "very religious" are 42 percent less likely to divorce than those who never attend worship services.

Jesus offers regeneration and the forgiveness of sin for those who will trust Him (Titus 3:5; John 5:24). Jesus offers a new beginning to those who are struggling with failure in their marriage. Paul said, "I can do all things through Him who strengthens me" (Philippians 4:13). Christ's strength is available to help make your marriage successful, joyous, and lasting.

And What About Love?

Have we missed something? Most people think of love as the most essential ingredient in a marriage. It is noticeably absent from our list. Isn't love essential to marriage?

Solomon declared, "Many waters cannot quench love, nor will rivers overflow it" (Song of Solomon 8:7). Love is not so much an ingredient as it is the result of having the right ingredients for a lasting and meaningful marriage. The unquenchable love of which Solomon spoke is the sweet fruit of a marriage relationship made with the proper recipe. Love is the result of growing and working together to develop a God-honoring marriage.

Marriages need not end in divorce. The ingredients shared here may serve as a checklist for evaluating and strengthening your marriage.

Some dear friends who have been a part of my church in past years recently celebrated their seventieth anniversary, Lowell and Eleanor Lawry. This lovely couple has spent seventy years together—seventy years of shared joys and sorrows. Seventy years! I have another twenty-five years to go before I reach that mark. Will I make it? Will you?

The ingredients make all the difference. Kool-Aid will never substitute for Jell-O. If we have the right ingredients, our marriages can be fulfilling and successful.

Study and Review Questions

1. How would you evaluate the following statements?
   - (a) Marriage is a fifty-fifty relationship.
   - (b) Marriage is a contract agreement.
   - (c) Love is the most essential ingredient for marriage.
   - (d) Some people just fall out of love.
   - (e) I don't want to be in a marriage with problems.
   - (f) If the marriage doesn't work, we can just get a divorce and try again.
2. Can you suggest a definition of marriage? What elements would be essential to a biblical marriage?
3. Why is sharing in spiritual life important to a lasting marriage?
4. Take some time to evaluate your own marriage. Consider each of these ten ingredients. Where is your marriage strong? Where might it need strengthening?
5. Together with your spouse, select an area of your marriage that needs some special attention. Talk about it. Decide on a positive course of action to help build this area of your marriage relationship.

Chapter 8
LOVING YOUR SPOUSE SEXUALLY

Many marital failures can be directly attributed to sexual dissatisfaction in marriage. And sexual dissatisfaction often results from a misunderstanding of the place and purpose of sex in marriage. Our attitude toward sex can make the difference between marital success and failure.

How should we view sex? Should married couples enjoy sexual intimacies as a wholesome, God-ordained gift? Or should sex be regarded as a necessary function to quench passion and obey God's command to "fill the earth" (Genesis 1:28)?

Some sober-minded Christians have regarded the mutual enjoyment of sex in marriage as somewhat unspiritual. They are a lot like the old spinster who tasted ice cream for the first time. After one bite she put down her spoon and declared, "It tastes so good, it must be sinful!" Many well-meaning and sincere Christians have said essentially the same thing about sex.

In his *Confessions*, St. Augustine, bishop of Hippo (A.D. 354-430), wrote that marital intercourse for the sake of mutual enjoyment constituted a "venial sin"![14] Another church father declared, "Anyone who is too passionate a lover with his own wife is himself an adulterer."

The sexual asceticism that permeated the thinking of many personalities of early church history reached its crescendo in the Middle Ages when the convents and monasteries flourished. The sex-sin syndrome is still reflected in the unbiblical attitudes many people hold regarding the physical expression of love in marriage.

The Wisdom Books shed considerable light on the subject of sex in marriage. Here we learn what attitudes couples should cultivate to make their marriages successful—pleasurable, satisfying, and enduring.

---

[14] Augustine, Confessions 2.3, *On Marriage and Concupiscence*, 1.1 6.

The Wholesomeness of Sex

We don't have to look too far to discover that Israel's sages viewed sex in marriage as a good, healthy, pleasurable gift from God. Solomon declares:

Let your fountain be blessed, and rejoice in the wife of your youth.

As a loving hind and a graceful doe, let her breasts satisfy you at all times;

Be exhilarated always with her love. (Proverbs 5:18-19). The Bible is quite forthright in declaring the wholesomeness of sex in the marriage relationship.

God created man and woman as sexual beings (Genesis 1:27). The words *male* and *female* are sexual terms and literally mean "the piercer" and "the pierced." Eve was created as the perfect physical counterpart to Adam. After creating man and woman as sexual beings, God evaluated His creation as "very good" (Genesis 1:31). Adam and Eve sensed no embarrassment over their sexuality. We read, "And the man and his wife were both naked and were not ashamed" (2:25).

Sex was God's idea from the beginning. The physical attraction between a man and a woman, and the expression of sexual intimacies in marriage, must be viewed as a natural, healthy, and wholesome endowment. The wholesomeness of sex is reflected in many scriptural passages (Genesis 2:24; Matthew 19:5; 1 Corinthians 7:2-5; Hebrews 13:4), and especially in the Song of Solomon (1:13-17; 2:5-6, 8-17; 4:1-6, 11-16; 5:1, 10-16; 7:1-9, 10-12; 8:3).

The Purposes of Sex

Sexual relations in marriage may be likened to a dazzling, multifaceted gem. As the beauty of a polished gem can be appreciated from several points of view, so it is with marital relations. Sex in marriage can be appreciated from the perspective of its five basic purposes.

Biological. Sex was designed by God as a means of procreation (Genesis 1:28). The word procreate means "to create for." In procreation the husband and wife share in God's creative activity as they together bring forth new life. To say that God designed sex for procreation does not imply that "making babies" is its only purpose. But it does suggest that when pregnancy results, such a condition ought not to be considered an "accident." When a couple shares a sexual union, they obligate themselves to accept mutual responsibility for the pregnancy that may result.

Re-creational. The sharing of sexual intimacies in a loving atmosphere serves to re-create the romantic feelings of love that fade so quickly in the busy activities and pressures of our twenty-first century world. The marriage relationship is refreshed, invigorated, and renewed by sharing together in the one-flesh relationship. Although husbands and wives are "one" apart from the sexual union, the experience of intercourse where their two bodies are pleasurably united restores the feelings of oneness once again.

Social. The sexual union is the most intense and concentrated expression of love possible between two human beings. As such, it is a vehicle for social interaction and self-giving. In marriage a husband gives himself to his wife and the wife gives herself to her husband (1 Corinthians 7:4). The partners give of themselves for the enjoyment and satisfaction of each other. The greatest fulfillment in sex comes from *giving* rather than receiving. The physical union provides opportunity for married persons to give satisfaction and enjoyment to each other.

Psychological. There is a psychological dimension to God's design for sex. For the better part of the day, husbands and wives function in different worlds. Sexual interest and desire serve to bring couples together— emotionally, psychologically, physically—after a day of different pursuits. God designed sexual relations as a magnetic attraction to minister to the couple's emotions. The physical relationship builds self-esteem, enhances one's sense of belonging, and brings a sense of security and fulfillment to the marriage.

Spiritual. Sex in marriage also has a spiritual purpose. Since marital intercourse is a vehicle for self-giving, it illustrates God's self-giving love for His people (John 3:16). In fact, the marriage union between a husband and wife is designed to portray the relationship between Christ and His church—an intimate and inseparable fellowship (Ephesians 5:31-32).

Exploring the Song of Solomon

More than any other of the Wisdom Books of the Bible, the Song of Solomon assists us in developing a proper attitude toward sex in marriage. The Hebrew title, "Song of Songs," is a superlative meaning, "The most excellent of songs." In other words, of the more than one-thousand songs Solomon wrote (1 Kings 4:32), this was regarded as his very best! Here Solomon teaches that love and physical attraction in marriage is not to be degraded but rather appreciated and even exalted. According to Solomon, sexual union is a beautiful gift that God wants married couples to fully enjoy.

The Song of Solomon is the Cinderella story of the Hebrew Bible. It is the story of a most unlikely relationship that blossoms into love and marriage.

King Solomon was Israel's richest king and owned vineyards all over the country. One of his vineyards was in the mountains of Lebanon (Song of Solomon 4:8; 8:11). It was entrusted to the care of a woman who had two sons (1:6) and two daughters (8:8). The oldest daughter is referred to in the Song as "the Shulammite," whom we will call "Shula."

Like Cinderella, Shula was required by her humble circumstances to do hard, manual labor. Long hours in the vineyard left her little opportunity to care for her own personal appearance (1:6). Working in the vineyard and keeping the flocks caused her skin to darken from the hot Palestinian sun (1:5).

One day, while caring for the vineyard, a stranger approached. Solomon may have been on a hunting trip. Mixing a little business with pleasure, he decided to check on his vineyard. Shula mistook the stranger for a shepherd and asked him about his flocks (1:7). Concealing his true identity, King Solomon spoke loving words to Shula (1:8-10). He wooed and won her to his heart. Solomon then departed, promising that he would one day return. Finally, he did return in all his kingly splendor to take Shula to Jerusalem to be his bride (3:6-7).

In his "most excellent song" Solomon poetically portrays the drama of his encounter with Shula. He tells of their love, courtship, marriage, and post-honeymoon adjustment. But the Song does more than memorialize a royal romance. It instructs us concerning the beauty and purity of the sexual expression of love in marriage.

Interpreting the Song of Solomon

There is no book in the Hebrew Bible that has found greater variety of interpretation than the Song of Solomon. Jewish rabbis have argued that the relationship between Solomon and Shula portrays God's relationship with Israel. Early Christians viewed the Song as describing Christ's love for the church.

Consider Shula's words addressed to Solomon, "My beloved is to me as a pouch of myrrh which lies all night between my breasts" (1:13). The rabbis interpreted this verse to refer to the Shekinah glory between the two cherubim that stood over the Ark in the Tabernacle. Early Christians understand this verse to refer to the coming of Christ ("the pouch of myrrh") between the Old and New Testament periods ("between my breasts").

Shula's statement, "I am black but lovely" (1:5) was interpreted to mean that Israel was black with sin because of making the golden calf at Mount Sinai, but had become "lovely" by receiving the Ten Commandments. Christians interpreted the verse to mean that believers were once black with sin, but have become lovely through the redemption provided by Christ.

How do we evaluate such approaches to the Song of Solomon? To me they appear artificial, extravagant, and forced. They are interpretations that involve reading something *into* the text instead of simply understanding the message God placed there for us.

I am suggesting that we interpret the Song in the normal (or literal) way, as we would any other piece of poetic literature. We should follow the customary, socially acknowledged meaning of a word or phrase. The Song of Solomon is a poetic portrayal of the deep love between a man and a woman. Illustrating the beauty and purity of marital intimacies, the Song helps us develop a biblical attitude regarding sexual relations in marriage.

Surveying the Song of Solomon

The Song of Solomon is full of lessons for married couples. But we will discover that there is also a message for single people. Before we consider those lessons, it would be helpful to explore the drama as it is presented in this amazing little book.

It is important to recognize at the outset that, while the book contains several "flashbacks" to his courtship days with Shula, Solomon wrote from the perspective of his consummated marriage. Although the wedding was not recalled and recorded until 4:7-5:1, chronologically it takes place before the first verse of chapter one.

The Mutual Affection of the Bride and Groom (1:1-2:7).
The Song begins with a dialogue that sets forth the mutual affection of Solomon and Shula. The first scene is in the king's palace where Shula expresses her love for King Solomon, but is self-conscious of her physical appearance compared to the other women in the royal palace (1:2-8). Shula is encouraged by the court maidens that she is indeed "most beautiful among women."

In the second scene, at the king's banquet table (1:9-14), Solomon praised the Shulammite's beauty and she returned his praise. In the third scene, we find the couple in their bridal chamber (1:15-2:7). Solomon praised his wife's physical attractiveness. Shula responded to Solomon, expressing her desire for sexual intimacies. The scene closes with the first of three warnings against awakening sexual passion prematurely (2:7).

The New Bride Reflects on Courtship and Marriage (2:8-3:5). In the next section, Solomon's new bride reflected on the romance of courtship as compared with the realities of marriage. Shula recalled her first meeting with Solomon. She was but a shy, country maiden. Solomon drew her out and they enjoyed a romantic springtime together.

But as with many young brides, the realities of marriage did not match up with the romance of courtship. Busy tending to royal duties, Solomon often left Shula sitting alone in the palace. She had a recurring dream of being separated from Solomon and unable to find him (3:1). Desiring more companionship with her husband, Shula determined that she would overcome this early difficulty in her marriage.

The Wedding of Solomon and the Shulammite (3:6-5:1). Following traditional Jewish custom, Solomon came for his bride at her home in Lebanon and brought her back to his palace in Jerusalem. Solomon was described in all his kingly splendor by the court maidens as they observed the bridal procession nearing Jerusalem (3:9-11).

In the next scene (4:1-5:1), Shula reflects on the events of her wedding night. She remembers how Solomon extolled her beauty before consummating their relationship. As chapter five begins, the bridal couple appears to be enjoying the "afterglow" of their becoming one flesh together. As the scene closes, God Himself expresses His approval of their physical relationship. "Eat, friends; drink and imbibe deeply, O lovers" (5:1b). God is encouraging Solomon and Shula to drink deeply of His gift of sexual love.

The Early Days of Marriage and Adjustment (5:2-6:13). Solomon's many responsibilities as king prevented him from spending as much time with Shula as she would have liked. Reacting to this situation, Shula became resentful and disinterested in sex. She dreamed of refusing Solomon entrance into her bedchamber (5:2-7). But then, her feelings were aroused and she opened the door—only to find him gone.

Realizing how she had been treating Solomon, Shula went about Jerusalem, looking for her husband. She eventually found in in his garden (5:9-6:3). There the lovers are reunited.

The Enjoyment of Sexual Love in Marriage (7:1-8:4). Solomon and Shula were alone in the palace. There Shula aggressively takes the initiative to arouse her husband by dancing before him. She wanted Solomon to gaze upon her and become sexually stimulated.

As they lay together after lovemaking, Shula asked Solomon to take her on a retreat in the country where they could enjoy each other without distraction (7:10-13). Shula expressed her desire for a closer relationship with Solomon. She wanted to spent time with him and enjoy a more intimate relationship (8:1-13).

The Visit to Shula's Country Home (8:5-14). Leaving the busy routine of royalty in the Jerusalem palace, Solomon and Shula traveled to the country for a time of rest, refreshment, and marriage enrichment. As they walked together, they viewed familiar places and recalled significant moments from the past.

Shula spoke with Solomon about her premarital virtue and her submission to Solomon in marriage (8:10-12). She was totally Solomon's. Shula had promised that on their retreat to the country she would give Solomon her love. In

the conclusion of the book, she fulfills that promise
(8:14).[15]

Applying the Song of Solomon

The Song of Solomon illustrates a number of practical
lessons, especially with regard to the sexual aspects of
marriage. Let's consider some of the exciting truths that we
discover in this biblical "marriage manual."

1. Married couples should not be hesitant to communicate
their appreciation of each other's physical attractiveness
(1:15-16). While the priority must be on the "hidden person
of the heart" (1 Peter 3:3-4), married couples should not
neglect the physical aspect of their relationship. God
created men and women as sexual beings and declared
His creation "very good" (Genesis 1:31).

2. Desire for sexual intimacies in marriage is healthy and
good. Solomon and Shula quite freely expressed such
desires (2:6,14; 8:3). Not only is it God's design for couples
to desire sex in marriage; the loving communication of that
desire is completely appropriate.

3. Love for one's spouse should be expressed tangibly
(1:11). An occasional gift, card, or bouquet of flowers
means a great deal to a woman. Some time ago, I
surprised my wife with a special gift. She knows that I love
her, because I tell her so. But the tangible expression of
my affection is reassuring and greatly appreciated.

4. The husband should recognize his role as leader and
initiator in the marriage relationship. Notice how Solomon
initiated the courtship (2:10-13) and romance (2:14).
Failure to take such initiative can result in a leadership

---

[15] For a more in depth exposition of the Song of Solomon, see David
Balsley, *The Passionate Prince: A Pastoral Exposition of the Song of
Solomon* (Westbow Press, 2015).

vacuum in the marriage and possible role reversal as the wife assumes more her husband's responsibility.

5. The husband must prepare his wife to respond to him sexually. Notice the progressive activity in Solomon's romance—a loving look, a quite walk, a sensuous suggestion . . . and a responsive lover (2:9-17). All that a man does for his wife by way of kindness and consideration throughout the day prepares her emotionally to respond to him as a lover. A good friend once told me that vacuuming the house for his wife was "foreplay." His helpfulness in cleaning the house prepared her for lovemaking.

6. A wife needs companionship with her husband (3:1-2). A wife should be her husband's best friend. This kind of companionship is especially important for wives who spend most of their day at home with children. A husband should avoid being so busy with his work or ministry that his wife feels separated or isolated. A wise husband will involve his wife in his work, ministry, and hobbies. This special relationship ought to be a sacred priority.

7. Expressions of appreciation for a spouse's physical beauty prepares the couple emotionally for lovemaking. Solomon praised Shula's beauty and stimulated her with kisses (4:1-6,11). Loving words, gentle hugs, and tender caresses are important preludes to sexual union. Notice, husbands, that Solomon was a gentleman. He did not force himself on his wife. But by his thoughtful preparation for their sexual encounter, he led Shula to respond.

8. God gives his blessing on sex in marriage. On their wedding night after the newly married couple had consummated their union, someone spoke and said to the newly wedding couple, "Eat, friends; drink and imbibe deeply, O lovers" (5:1b). Who was it? I suggest these are God's words of blessing on the couple and their newly discovered intimacy in marriage. God created sex as a

beautiful gift. Those who are married have His blessing to enjoy this gift to the fullest.

9. Sexual rejection damages marriage relationships. Recall Shula's dream about Solomon's coming to her after she had retired for the evening. Resentful of his neglect, she rejected him (5:2-8). Although this was a dream, many husbands can identify with Solomon's frustration over Shula's resistance to lovemaking. Paul addressed this issue when he pointed out that a wife does not have authority over her own body, but her husband does (1 Corinthians 7:3-5). Similarly, the husband does not have authority over his own body, but his wife does. Giving oneself physically in marriage is a sacred privilege. In this way husbands and wives are able to minister to each other as no other person can.

10. Maintain a sense of humor, even in the midst of marital difficulties. Solomon did not allow Shula's rebuff to suppress his expressions of love and praise. After he sensed Shula's anger over his neglect, Solomon said, "You are as beautiful as Tirzah, my darling, as lovely as Jerusalem, as awesome as an army with banners!" (6:4).

11. Don't take inhibitions into the bedroom. Sexual expression need not be subject to inhibitions or embarrassment in the privacy of one's bedroom. Gazing upon the disrobed Shula, Solomon described her body in loving detail (7:1-9). Like Adam and Eve, they were naked and not ashamed (Genesis 2:25).

12. Marriage enrichment retreats are essential to strengthening a relationship. From time to time, every married couple needs to pull away from the affairs of business, ministry, and children to develop and strengthen their relationship. Shula said, "Come, my beloved, let us go out into the country .... There I will give you my love" (7:11-2). These retreats refresh and renew our relationships and create memories of special intimate times shared together.

13.   The last section of the Song teaches a great lesson on the nature of genuine love (8:8-7). Solomon said, "Many waters cannot quench love, nor will rivers overflow it." His love for Shula is described as "strong as death." It's binding and permanent. The kind of love Solomon is writing about is not a feeling; it is a dynamic force that grows and develops into intense, personal commitment. Love is not something we can "fall out" of. It is invincible and cannot be quenched by sin, sorrow or sickness. Love is not something that can be bought for a price. It can only be freely given.

14.   You may be wondering, "How can I experience this kind of love in my marriage?" The key to developing the kind of love featured in the Song of Solomon is to follow the pattern set by Jesus. He said, "Love one another even as I have loved you (John 13:34). Jesus loved unconditionally—while we were yet sinners. Jesus loved sacrificially—even to death on a cross. This is the pattern of love that lays the foundation for a satisfying sexual relationship and a successful marriage.

Study and Review Questions
1. What has been your attitude toward sex? Have you viewed sex in a positive or negative light? What have been the major influences, secular and religious, upon your attitude toward sex.
2. How do the Wisdom writers regard sex? Do they distinguish between a proper use and a misuse of sex?
3. According to Scripture, what context did God design sexual intimacies to be enjoyed. How does the Song of Solomon 2:7; 3:5; and 8:4 help your thinking in this regard.
4. What are the major purposes of sex? Are there any you would add to the ones mentioned in this chapter. Which of these major purposes are most important to you at this time in your life?

5. What is the historical background of the Song of Solomon? Can you relate the story behind the song?
6. How has the Song of Solomon been interpreted in the past? What approach do you take? Can you explain why?
7. Which of these lessons in the Song of Solomon has had the greatest impact on your thinking about sex?

Chapter 9
FACING THE CHALLENGE OF PARENTING

The search for success goes on. And, thankfully, our efforts are not in vain. God's Word reveals that "wisdom has the advantage of giving success." If consistently applied, the wise precepts of Israel's sages will enable God's people to live successfully, avoiding unnecessary pitfalls, getting the most out of life, and being a blessing to others.

The biblical wisdom writers give considerable attention to parenting, one of the greatest of life's challenges. For me, it all began at 2:00 AM on November 24, 1976. That's when my wife Nancy nudged me and said, "Honey, this is it!"

I pulled myself out of a deep sleep, realizing that Nancy was in labor. Although I did not fully realize it at the time, I was about to enter a period of major life change. For the previous five years Nancy and I had enjoyed our marriage as a couple. Now we were becoming a family.

After about ten hours of labor, the grand moment finally arrived. I'll never forget the pride and joy I felt as the doctor said, "It's a boy," and gently held up our pink little baby. After being wrapped in warm blankets, the nurse laid John Carl III in my arms and I carried that little bundle to the hospital nursery. After a short visit with Nancy, I was off to tell the world that our baby had been born.

Since the birth of my son, and later two daughters and another son, I have known the joy, delight, pride, anxiety, frustration, and sense of helplessness that comes with being a parent. I have prayed more, loved more, and learned more in these years than any previous period of my life.

Being a parent can be a source of great joy. But it can also be a cause for anxiety. "Is there life after parenthood?"

one may ask. How can parents cope successfully with the challenges they face?

Fortunately, parenting is nothing new. Most of the wise teachers of ancient Israel were parents. In the Wisdom Books they offer some helpful advice for those who want to rear their children successfully.

Discovering God's Perspective

When my wife, Nancy, first suspected that she was pregnant, she went to a medical clinic to have the condition confirmed. Before the nurse reported the results of the test, she asked, "Do you view pregnancy as a good thing or a bad thing?"

"What do you mean?" Nancy queried.

"I mean," replied the nurse, "do you want to go through with it? Do you want to have the baby?"

As a matter of routine procedure, Nancy was offered the option of aborting our unborn child. Undoubtedly, many of the women who came to that clinic chose abortion instead of childbirth. This view of children and family life stands in stark contrast with the attitude expressed in the Bible.

The family was the first institution God created (Genesis 2:23-24). It existed long before the establishment of Israel, the temple worship, or the church. According to God's Word, the family is important. And its importance must be recognized by those seeking wisdom and success in life.

Many twenty-first century couples have come to view children as a hindrance to their careers. They want to enjoy life with the freedom pursue their careers and to travel without having children consuming their time and resources. The sages of Israel viewed this quite differently. Solomon said, "Behold, children are a gift of the LORD; the fruit of the womb is a reward. Like arrows in the hand of a warrior, so are the children of one's youth. How blessed is the man whose quiver is full of them" (Psalm 127:3-5). According to the psalmist, having many children is an evidence of God's great blessing (128:1-4).

Children are important to God because He creates them. God is the One who opens the womb and allows conception (Genesis 29:33; 30:22). He is personally and intimately involved in the formation of the unborn child in the womb (Psalm 139:13-16).

The importance of the family can be seen by the fact that God established it as the first and foremost educational institution. Back in Eden, God didn't provide priests, pastors, or Sunday school teachers. There were no temples, synagogues, or churches. Yet, there was a learning center—the home.

In the earliest biblical period, spiritual truth was communicated through the family. Moses commanded parents to teach their children (Deuteronomy 6:1-3, 20-25). In Proverbs, fathers and mothers are urged to train their children (10:1; 15:20; 29:3). Children are commanded to obey parental instruction (1:1; 4:1, 3-4; 6:20-23).

The Bible reveals that the spiritual welfare and instruction of children is a *parental* responsibility. Certainly Sunday school can help. But God has placed the primary responsibility for the spiritual development of children squarely on the shoulders of parents. If I am successful as a teacher, preacher, and writer, but fail to train my children in the truth of God's Word, I have failed in my most important ministry. That's God's perspective.

Priorities for Parents

Establishing priorities allows us to give our greatest attention to those things that are most important. Every day I must set priorities in order to fulfill my responsibilities in the classes I teach. Will I answer this letter or prepare the midterm exam? To be ready tomorrow, the exam must be printed today. So it takes a place of priority on my list of things to do.

We who are parents must establish priories as well. By so doing, we will be able to give time and attention to matters that will have the most significant, long-term impact on the lives of our children. By providing us with an eternal perspective, the wisdom writers of Israel help parents establish priorities.

The Most Important Inheritance. The most important inheritance a parent can pass on to a child is a spiritual heritage. Kind David issued an invitation, "Come, you children, listen to me; I will teach you the fear of the LORD" (Psalm 34:11). If I provide my children with a cozy home, educational toys, piano lessons, and a college education, but don't impart to them the spiritual truth that has vitalized my own life, then I have not fulfilled my duty as a parent.

Often there is a decline in spirituality from one generation to the next. Someone has said, "To our forefathers, their faith was an experience. To our fathers, their faith was an inheritance. To us, our faith is a convenience. To our children, faith is a nuisance." How, then, is our spiritual heritage to be passed on?

A spiritual heritage can't be provided simply through weekly family devotions and evening prayers, as good and helpful as these activities are. A spiritual heritage is provided as parents incorporate their own faith into their daily lives and activities in such a way as to demonstrate to their children that knowing God makes a real difference in their lives.

When my children hear their mother pray for issues that concern our family and see those prayers answered, they learn a great truth. Prayer works! God is concerned about the matters that concern us. He is concerned about the details of our lives. Our relationship with God is not just a Sabbath or Sunday worship experience, but a personal, daily walk with the living God. Living our faith before the lives of our children will enable them to witness the genuine, spiritual vitality of one who walks with God. And they will be encouraged to claim this heritage for themselves.

The Most Important Teaching Opportunity. The most important teaching opportunity a parent will ever have is in the home. Solomon set forth the wisdom of teaching our children and the serious consequences if failing to do so. He said, "A wise son makes his father glad, but a foolish son is a grief to his mother" (Proverbs 10:1; 15:20; 29:3).

According to Solomon, a parent's teaching will serve to guide and direct the child into the path of light and life (6:20-24).

Solomon recalled his father David's instruction early in his childhood. "When I was a son to my father, tender and the only son in the sight of my mother, then he taught me and said to me, 'Let your heart hold fast my words; keep my commandments and live'" (Proverbs 4:3-4).

Parents should teach their children not only spiritual truths, but lessons about work, finance, time, friendship, commitment, and morality. The curriculum is staggering and the teaching load is heavy, but the long-term rewards are many. Well-trained children will give their parents occasion to rejoice (Proverbs 23:24-25). On the other hand, "The father of a fool has no joy" (17:21).

The Most Important Task. The most important task a parent has is laying a solid foundation for the child's future years. The time for a parent's input into the life of a child is quite limited. After the teenage years, most children are on their own, independent of parents' direct control and influence. For many children, the apron strings are cut even sooner.

As much as parents might like to guide their child through all of life's important decisions, there is no way this would be feasible. Nor would it be wise. But what parents can do is help the child lay a solid foundation for decision making in the future. As the foundation is the most important part of a building, so the early years are the most important part of life. During the early years, parents may impart values, beliefs, and attitudes that will enable the child to become a successful and productive person.

Solomon stressed the importance of laying a foundation in the early years. "Train up a child in the way he should go, even when he is old he will not depart from it" (Proverbs 22:6). Some have taken this verse as a promise that a child who goes to Sunday school may turn from the Lord and "sow some wild oats," but will turn back to the Lord when he or she matures as an adult.

This interpretation represents more wishful thinking than sound exposition. What Solomon was emphasizing was that there are strategic opportunities for positive training and instruction during the childhood years. The lessons learned during these formative years will serve as guideposts during adult life.

The phrase, "In the way he should go," literally reads, "according to his way" and points to a parental concern for the child's individuality, interests, and pursuits. A wise parent will recognize a child's inclinations and use these early years to confirm, correct, and encourage the building of a solid foundation.

The Most Important Means of Training. The most important means of training children is by personal example. A frustrated parent will sometimes bark, "So as I say, not as I do!" When a father teaches the importance of submission to civil authorities, but drives seventy-five miles per hour in a sixty mile-per-hour zone and cheats on his income tax, his children learn that it is OK to be a two-faced hypocrite. The teaching by word is cancelled out by the teaching by example.

In Proverbs we read, "A righteous man who walks in his integrity—how blessed are his sons after him" (20:7). Great blessing in the lives of children is just one of the many positive results that come from the presence of a godly example in the home.

Someone has said that the two most important gifts parents can give their children are "roots and wings." *Roots* refers to the confidence built by unconditional love, encouragement, and spiritual training. *Wing*s refers to the freedom to be an individual person, unencumbered by the wishes and expectations of parents. As parents, we must keep a good sense of humor, bring our children before the Lord daily in prayer, and seek to impart to them deep roots and strong wings.

Disciplining Your Children

I remember as a child being given the sobering task of having to fetch a switch, which was then to be applied with vigor to my legs and bottom. Being disciplined wasn't much fun. As the writer of Hebrews said, "All discipline for the moment seems not to be joyful, but sorrowful" (12:11). Then he added, "Yet to those who have been trained by it, afterwards it yields the peaceful fruit of righteousness." I, too, have experienced the fruitful results of discipline in my own life. While I didn't relish it at the time, I am grateful today for the loving and consistent discipline administered by my parents.

When someone mentions discipline, most of us think primarily of physical discipline. The biblical concept, however, is much broader (Proverbs 29:15). Biblical discipline is simply training—training by *word* (Proverbs 15:32; Psalm 50:17) and training by *deed* (Proverbs 13:34; 23:13). Training by word involves education, reminders, warnings, and gentle rebukes. Training by deed involves both corrective and preventative discipline.

When a child disobeys your clear instruction not to cross the street alone, discipline must be applied. Similarly, when a child cleans up his or her room at your request, there should be some positive reinforcement of that good behavior. Most parents are aware of the need to carry out corrective discipline, but often neglect preventative discipline. The latter involves listening to your children, playing with them, and spending time developing a relationship in which obedience is encouraged and motivated by love (John 14:15).

Corrective discipline (punishment for wrongdoing) takes place on the spur of the moment and requires little planning. *Preventive* discipline takes forethought, time, and commitment. It is hard to justify taking time for discipline when all is well. But it has been my experience that corrective discipline without regular preventative discipline is frustrating, futile, and fails to change a child's behavior.

When our second daughter was born, there was a significant change in the behavior of our middle child. She was apparently attempting to win back the attention she felt she was being deprived of by the presence of the new baby. In spite of our attempts to compensate for this and meet her need, she became whiny, disobedient, and generally difficult. Physical discipline was becoming less and less effective. We needed a new tactic.

One day I invited my daughter to have lunch at my office. Sometime later I took her trout fishing. On another occasion I took her shopping and bought her some new socks and underclothes. The improvement in her behavior did not take place overnight. There were ups and downs. But preventive discipline coupled with corrective discipline was effective in helping our daughter become a sweet little girl again. We must not over-emphasize physical discipline to the neglect of developing a relationship with the child that encourages and rewards obedience.

Physical discipline is an essential aspect of child training. Solomon says, "Do not hold back discipline from the child, although you beat him with the rod, he will not die. You shall beat him with the rod, and deliver his soul from *Sheol* [the grave]" (Proverbs 23:13-14). Proverbs makes repeated reference to the use of physical discipline in child training (13:24; 20:30; 22:15). Yet these verses don't give parents a license to be abusive. They simply reflect a biblical perspective on child rearing which includes physical discipline administered with gentleness and love.

There are other kinds of discipline as well. Our desire for peace and quiet in the home may lead us to prefer preventive and instructive discipline. Yet as much as parents might like to avoid the crying and tears associated with spankings, physical discipline is biblical and must be applied in some child-training situations.

Note that I said *some* situations, not all. Spankings are the ultimate act in child discipline and ought to be reserved for coldhearted acts of defiance, disobedience, and rebellion against parental authority. Children should not be spanked for accidentally spilling their milk, wetting their beds, or failing to finish their dinner. But when a child is given explicit directions and responds, "No, I won't," then that child's defiance of the parent's authority may indicate that physical discipline has become necessary.

Biblical discipline must be motivated by love. On occasion a parent may succumb to disciplining a child out of anger and frustration. But love is what motivates God's discipline and that is the proper motivation for the parent. "For whom the LORD loves, He reproves, even as a father, the son in whom he delights" (Proverbs 3:12). Elsewhere Solomon declared, "He who spares his rod hates his son, but he who loves him disciplines him diligently" (Proverbs 13:34).

How can a parent discipline a child in love? *First*, by dealing with one's own anger before carrying out discipline. One should never spank a child out of anger. *Second*, a parent should explain to the child the reason for the discipline. A parent should call attention to the fact that the act of defiance is unacceptable and does not please God. *Third*, disciplining in love means telling the child that it is because of the parent's great love and concern that the discipline must be carried out. *Fourth*, it can be done by offering comfort and assurance of the parent's love as the proper follow-up for discipline. The times after love-motivated discipline are some of the sweetest moments I have shared with my children. Dr. James Dobson said that the best opportunity to communicate with a child often occurs after discipline.[16]

Discipline may take different forms in different situations and stages in life. A spanking isn't the answer to every discipline problem. I raised a very active child who found it difficult to "turn her motor off" at night. She would lie in bed for hours, totally exhausted, but unable to go to sleep. She would sometimes get up three, four, and five times before dozing off at last. I tried various forms of discipline, including spankings, but nothing I did would resolve the situation.

---

[16] James Dobson, *Dare to Discipline* (Wheaton, Ill.; Tyndale House Publishers, 1970), p. 35.

Then I began to view my role as a parent more in terms of meeting my child's needs. My daughter's need was to relax. So after putting her back in bed several times on evening, I told her to lie quietly in bed and that I would rub her back. She lay very still, enjoying the back rub, and was asleep in minutes.

Parents should be encouraged to reserve spankings for young children. It is during the formative years of two to seven that a spanking is most effective. After the age of seven or eight, I would suggest the use of other kinds of discipline—taking "time outs," forfeiting a week's allowance, or losing computer or television privileges.

By the time a child is a teenager, spankings need to be totally eliminated from a parent's list of disciplinary procedures. There is nothing more devastating to a teenager's self-esteem than the humiliation of a spanking. Withhold driving privileges, require a Saturday workday at home, cancel a weekend outing, but don't spank your teenager. For a teen, a spanking is "the ultimate insult."

Bear in mind that every child is different and will respond to some forms of discipline better than others. My oldest son responded well to corrective (physical) discipline. But this wasn't as effective with my other children. Some children need more corrective discipline. Others seem to learn from the mistakes of their siblings and require less. While I have emphasized the place of physical discipline in this chapter, I want to conclude by urging caution. If you choose to including spankings among your options, make sure you exercise your discipline with love and care, not with anger or malice.

Measuring Your Success

Like most parents, I have felt the disappointment of following all the right biblical principles and not seeing the positive results in the lives of my own children. What has gone wrong? Why is there no improvement in the child's behavior?

Often such a disappointment is the result of focusing on the immediate payoff rather than the long-term effect. We have worked hard and want to see the results. But kids are still kids and much of their misbehavior must be attributed to immaturity.

It would be better to measure our success in parenting by our faithful application of the biblical principles, leaving the ultimate outcome to God. Have we trained our children spiritually? Have we disciplined them consistently? Have we prayed for them faithfully? Have we made parenting a priority? If we can answer "yes," then we have been successful as parents. We have cultivated the ground, sown the seed, and pulled the weeds. Now, we must trust the Lord to bring for the fruit of our labor.

My wife, Nancy, and I have raised our four children to adulthood. And quite honestly, raising four kids is the hardest thing we have ever done! I found that raising kids is infinitely harder than writing a book, preparing a lecture, teaching a class, or preaching a sermon. But by God's grace, Nancy and I survived the experience and our kids have turned out OK. During their early, rebellious years I sometimes feared that I was raising juvenile delinquents who would end up in jail! But we did our best to show them lots of love and follow biblical principles of discipline, and now our children are wonderful, young adults raising their own children. I look back and thank God for guiding Nancy and I as parents and extending His grace to our children.

Now as grandparents, we seek to encourage young parents that in spite of the challenges and occasional setbacks, they are doing OK. By demonstrating lots of love and following the biblical principles of child rearing, they will be successful as parents.

Study and Review Questions
1. What evidence is there from Scripture that God has a high regard for family life?
2. What perspective does the Bible offer in regard to children? What place do they have in the family?
3. What priorities do you see as essential to being a successful parent?

4. Why is it that young people often abandon their faith that was presented to them in their childhood years?
5. What does the Bible mean by the word discipline? Distinguish between corrective and preventive discipline.
6. What specific methods of corrective discipline would you use and recommend.

Chapter 10
Worshiping in the Spirit

We have learned that the "fear of the Lord" is the first lesson of wisdom, and that wisdom yields success. So, to practice the fear of the Lord would be to apply wisdom, and then to experience the outcome—success. According to the wisdom writers, a genuine reverence for God is one of the distinguishing characteristics of a truly successful person.

Worship is a subject that usually kindles little interest among many of God's people. The reason may be that our definition of worship is too limited. Perhaps we have never experienced worship as God intended it.

One of my colleagues asked me to join him for a day of fly fishing on the Crooked River, a stream in Oregon noted for its wild rainbow trout. Knowing it would be my last chance of the season to go fishing, I accepted his invitation.

The day was absolutely delightful. The morning air was crisp, and the sky was a brilliant blue. The fragrance of juniper and sage filled the desert air. Rugged cliffs towered high above the riverbank. As I fished, I enjoyed watching two bald eagles riding the air currents along the cliffs.

After a leisurely lunch, I stretched out for a nap in the warm fall sunshine. What a day! No phone calls; no emails to answer; no lectures to prepare; no schedule to keep. There was nothing to do but fish and enjoy the beauty of God's creation.

I caught just two medium-sized trout during the day, but I wasn't disappointed. The day had been perfect. As the afternoon grew late and the sun cast a pink glow on the river gorge, I was simply overwhelmed with the magnificence of the scene before me. Standing in the river with my fishing rod in hand I prayed, "Lord, I just want to pause and worship You. The majesty of Your creative power is beautifully displayed in this place. I want You to know how much I appreciate Your revelation in nature."

My prayer was interrupted as I felt a powerful tug on my line. Strike! I knew in a moment that it was no average trout. Keeping my line taut, I eventually coaxed a seventeen-inch rainbow into my net. It was as if the Lord was saying, "Carl, I accept your worship and appreciation of My artwork in creation. Here is a little something to add to your enjoyment of this day."

What a day! What a God! What a worship experience! Many of us may have had such memorable moments of worship. For others our worship experiences have been as dry as sawdust, stale as old cornflakes.

If we are to be successful, we must be successful at worship, so we should learn to make it a more meaningful and enjoyable experience.

A Definition of Worship

The English word *worship* is derived from the Anglo-Saxon *weorthscipe*, which became *worthship*, and eventually *worship*. The background of the English term suggests that worship involves attributing "worth" to God. The Hebrew term used to denote worship literally means "to bow down" or "to prostrate oneself." The act of bowing is intended to reflect one's acknowledgment of God's worth. The gesture of bowing is reflected in many New Testament references that mention "bending the knee" (Luke 22:41; Philippians 2:10). The term used most frequently in the New Testament to denote worship literally means "to kiss toward." It reflects the ancient practice of kissing the earth as a means of honoring deities.

In their insightful book on worship, Ronald Allen and Gordon Borror offer a concise definition of worship. "Worship is an active response to God whereby we declare His worth."[17] They add, "Worship is not simply a mood; it is a response. Worship is not just a feeling; it is a declaration."[18] God's worth may be declared or acknowledged in many different ways—through song, thanksgiving, praise, prayer, or the reading of Scripture. It can take place in a public worship service or in the privacy of one's prayer closet. Worship is not a matter of mere outward form, but of inward attitude.

The concept of worship is illuminated by Jesus' conversation with the Samaritan woman (John 4). In an attempt to sidestep the issue of her sin, the woman raised a theological question regarding the proper location for worship. While the Samaritans regarded Mount Gerizim as the rightful worship center, the Jews held that God was to be worshiped only in Jerusalem.

Jesus pointed out to the woman that, in the past, worship had been focused on a place. But in the future, it would focus on a Person (John 4:21). Then Jesus added, "An hour is coming, and now is, when the true worshipers shall worship the Father in spirit and truth; for such people the Father seeks to be His worshipers. God is spirit, and those who worship Him must worship in spirit and truth" (John 4:23-24). What is meant by the phrase, "in spirit and truth?"

In Spirit. We have all caught ourselves daydreaming during worship. While singing hymns, we find ourselves thinking about Saturday's ball game. We are participating in the formalities of worship, but is this worship "in spirit."?

To worship "in spirit" is to worship after the pattern of God's essential nature. Since God is spirit, worship must be bound up with spiritual realities, not physical formalities.

---

[17] Ronald Allen and Gordon Borror, *Worship: Rediscovering the Missing Jewel* (Portland, Oregon: Multnomah Press, 1982), p. 16.
[18] Ibid.

The sages and prophets of the Hebrew Bible condemn religious externalism that is devoid of spiritual reality. God has little regard for mere formalities. David declared, "Sacrifice and meal offering You have not desired, . . . burnt offering and sin offering You have not required" (Psalm 40:6). Sacrificial worship, however elaborate, does not please God apart from a sincere love for His Person and commitment to His will (Hosea 6:6; Micah 6:6-8). Worship has more to do with the state of the *heart* than the state of the *art*.

Shakespeare's Hamlet acknowledged, "My words fly up, my thoughts remain below; words, without thoughts, never to heaven go"[19] God is not interested in our words of worship unless they express the genuine attitude of our hearts. David said, "The sacrifices of God are a broken spirit; a broken and a contrite heart, O God, You will not despise" (Psalm 51:17).

In Truth. To worship "in truth" means to worship the true God—the God of the Bible. It also means to value God because of who He is, not because of what He provides. Gresham Machen, defender of the faith and principle founder of Westminster Theological Seminary, wrote, "We are subject to many pressing needs, and we are too much inclined to value God, not for His own sake, but only because He can satisfy those needs."[20]

We live in a generation that is very utilitarian. We use things. We use people. We seem to want to use God, also. We sometimes worship God not for His own sake, but because we want something from Him, because we want to be "on his good side" and receive the benefits.

A seminary colleague suggested that I copyright the prayer that led to my catching the large rainbow trout. Then I could sell it to other fishermen! Dr. Ron Allen overheard the remark and interjected with a smile, "But

---

[19] William Shakespeare, *Hamlet*, III.111.97.
[20] J. Gresham Machen, *What is Faith?* (Grand Rapids: Wm. B. Eerdmans Publishing Co., 1946), p. 72

then the worship would not be *in truth*." Such worship would be motivated by a greedy desire to catch a fat fish. To worship "in truth" means to worship honestly, genuinely, and from the heart. It means to exalt God for who He is, not for what He gives.

Activities of Worship

Worship is not just an opportunity. It is a responsibility. Scripture records specific invitations or commands to worship. The imperative form of the verb is used to emphasize that worship is an activity, not just a topic for theological discussion.

The imperative of worship appears frequently in the Psalms. "Worship the LORD in holy array" (29:2). "Come, let us worship and bow down; let us kneel before the LORD our Maker" (95:6). "Exalt the LORD our God, and worship at His holy hill (99:9). "Let us go into His dwelling place, let us worship at His footstool" (132:7).

Jesus told the woman at Jacob's well that God the Father seeks those who will worship Him in spirit and truth. It is so easy to forget this priority.

Last Sunday morning I was sitting in the church service, weary from eight hours of teaching the day before. My wool jacket was warm and the pew was comfortable. Five minutes into the pastor's sermon my mind began to shift into neutral. My eyelids drooped…and then closed. I'm embarrassed to say that the next thing I knew was that the pastor was closing in prayer! I told myself that I had not *really* been sleeping, but the fact was, I couldn't remember a thing about the sermon! I had been given the opportunity to worship God in spirit and in truth, but I had missed it. I determined then and there that I would commit myself to being a *participant* in worship, not just a *bystander* at worship.

Psalm 100 is an invitation to worship. It suggests a core of activities that ought to be central to our worship experience. Let's consider each one.

Singing. The psalmist exhorts, "Serve the LORD with gladness; come before Him with joyful singing" (Psalm 100:2). Singing is a musical response to God whereby believers can declare His worth. Many of us hesitate to worship God in song for fear of missing a few notes or singing flat. While quality is not irrelevant (Psalm 33:3-4), what the psalmist emphasizes here is the attitude of the singer. Singing should be a joyful expression of worship.

Many worshipers, myself included, cannot sing parts or carry a melody. But we can sing with enthusiasm, sincerity, and joy in our hearts. It may not appeal to the musically trained ear, but from God's perspective, our singing is worship--if done in sincerity and truth.

Thanksgiving. The second worship activity mentioned in Psalm 100 is giving thanks. The psalmist invites worships to "enter His gates with thanksgiving" (100:4). The "gates" refer to the temple entrances. When the Israelites came into the temple area to celebrate the feasts and worship God, they were to come with words of thanksgiving on their lips.

The word translated "thanksgiving" means "to confess" and is used here as acknowledging God's character and works. In ancient Israel, when a worshiper presented a thank offering in the temple, there would be a public declaration of why the offering was being given. The worshiper would declare what God had done to elicit this worship. God's gracious benefits would be recited and His attributes declared.

While believers today are not involved in temple ritual, the writer of Hebrews insists that sacrifices of praise are still appropriate. "Through Him then, let us continually offer up a sacrifice of praise to God, that is, the fruit of lips that give thanks to His name" (Hebrews 13:15).

Many of the psalms in the Hebrew Bible were written by worshipers who had recently experienced God's saving deeds in their behalf. Desiring to honor God publicly, they wrote out their testimony and recited it before the other worshipers assembled in the temple. These testimonies were frequently set to music and sung in worship (Psalm 147:7).

One spring I had a unique opportunity to give thanks to God. I was involved in a bike accident that could have ended my life. That evening I wrote a psalm of thanksgiving which I later read during a chapel service at Western Seminary. My psalm illustrates how you can share an experience in your life to express thankful worship to God.

The Dark Night When I was Hit by the Truck

Give a shout of praise for our great God!
I came close to injury and maybe death,
but God delivered me completely.
I was bicycling to Western to teach my Monday night class.
At 62nd and Stark a truck came around the corner—fast!
The headlights were coming right toward me;
I knew they were going to hit me;
I could not get out of the way in time.
At the moment of impact, I leaped off the bicycle
And dove toward the curb.
The Lord enabled me to clear the hood of the truck
And to avoid injury in landing.
My bicycle was smashed hard
And the truck hit the curb opposite me.
But I was safe!
My first words were,
"Thank you, Lord, for keeping me alive!"
I will give public acknowledgment
Of what God has accomplished for me,
And how He delivered me from mishap!
Thanks be to our great God;
He does all things well!

When I concluded sharing my psalm in chapel, the students broke out in spontaneous applause. Following the exhortation of Psalm 47:1, they clapped their hands for joy! As I acknowledged His intervention in my behalf, God was exalted, magnified, and honored by those who heard.

Praising. A third form of worship mentioned in Psalm 100 is praise. "Enter His gates with thanksgiving, and His courts with praise" (100:4). Praise is an integral aspect of worship. The Hebrew title of the Psalms is literally, "Book of Praises." This word is related to an Arabic word that was the shout of triumph at the end of the battle, when the army had won and the booty was about to be divided.[21]

The most frequent use of "praise" was in connection with worshiping God. It is distinctive from the other words for worship in that it emphasizes boasting in the character and work of God. The psalmist declared, "Praise Him for His mighty deeds; praise Him according to His excellent greatness" (150:2).

I recall listening to my brother-in-law telling of taking a bull elk with a bow and arrow. He called in the elk with a bugle and by hitting branches against a tree trunk in imitation of an elk in rut, ready to battle for a choice cow. The elk fell on a steep mountainside and had to be roped in place while being gutted and field dressed. My brother-in-law spent the next two days packing the meat back to camp.

Alan enjoyed telling the story, especially since he was the only one of a party of ten hunters to tag an elk during the hunt. Now if we can allow such exulting in human accomplishments, how much more appropriate is it for us to boast in the great things of God. The psalmist encourages this by his words, "Praise Him for His mighty deeds!" (150:2).

---

[21] Ronald Barclay Allen, *Praise! A Matter of Life and Breath* (Nashville: Thomas Nelson Publishers, 1978), p. 64.

Blessing. The fourth activity mentioned in Psalm 100 is "blessing" God's name. "Give thanks to Him; bless His name" (100:4). The word *bless* appears to be derived from the Hebrew word for *knee*. In fact, the Hebrew verb *to bless* is sometimes translated "kneel" (Psalm 95:6). We bless God's name by acknowledging His character and attributes. We bless God's name when we submit to His authority and obey His will.

Further insight into what it means to "bless" the Lord is provided in Psalm 103:2 where David expressed his personal desire to worship God. He said, "Bless the LORD, O my soul, and forget none of His benefits." David then recited many of God's gracious benefits (103:3-5). To bless the Lord is to remember, and not forget, His saving deeds. There is a strong emphasis in Scripture on remembering what God has done. The psalmist declared, "I shall remember the deeds of the LORD, surely I will remember Your wonders of old."

Psalm 100 does not provide an exhaustive list of worship activities. Those who worship in spirit and truth must allow for spontaneity and creativity in the forms of worship. Worship may include the use of drama, audiovisual media, and group activity. One church devoted an evening service during the Christmas season to making advent wreaths. After each family had prepared a wreath, the spiritual significance of the advent season was explained. Christians can maintain a freshness in worship by using creative activities along with the more traditional forms to praise our great God.

Opportunities of Worship

Most of us equate worship with going to church. There is no scriptural basis for such a limited concept of worship. I suggest that there are three basic opportunities for worship.

Corporate. Corporate or congregational worship may take place at a religious service, school or hospital

131

chapel, or anywhere people gather for praise, prayer, or to read the Scriptures. Ancient Israel enjoyed corporate worship at the annual holy convocations or feasts (Leviticus 23). The corporate worship by God's people is reflected in Psalm 122:1, "I was glad when they said to me, 'Let us go to the house of the LORD.'"

Corporate worship is found in the New Testament as well. The Holy Spirit came at Pentecost when the disciples "were all together in one place" (Acts 2:1). Paul acknowledged the meeting of the corporate body in his correspondence to the Corinthians. He repeatedly used the phrase, "when you come together," when giving instructions about their gathering as a congregation (1 Corinthians 11:17-20; 33).

While worship may be celebrated through a variety of activities, corporate or congregational worship provides the best forum for praise. Praise is simply the public acknowledgment of God's attributes or activities. David said, "I will tell of Your name to my brethren; in the midst of the assembly I will praise You" (Psalm 22:22). "I will give You thanks in the great congregation; I will praise You among a mighty throng" (Psalm 35:18). We can pray in private, but praise must be done in public in order that God's reputation may be magnified in the sight of others.

Family. While there is no specific command in Scripture to worship as a family, the concept of family worship is found throughout the Hebrew Bible. In the biblical period, family worship took place on a regular basis as the Jews celebrated the Sabbath in their homes (Leviticus 23:3). The Sabbath (*Shabbat*) was to be a day of rest. But not *just* a day of rest. It was a day to remember God's works (Exodus 20:11; Deuteronomy 5:15) and delight in His person (Isaiah 58:13). Many of the feasts observed by Israel provided special opportunities for family worship.

In my opinion, family worship is the most important spiritual training parents can provide their children—not

Sunday school, junior church, Christian school or the Awana program. These activities may supplement family worship, but they can never replace the positive spiritual benefits that family worship offers. The importance of worship and spiritual training in the family context is highlighted in the Bible (Deuteronomy 6:1-9; 20-25). By emphasizing this in our homes today, we can instill in the next generation a more faithful commitment to God and an appreciation of His great benefits and blessings.

Family worship is an important part of my own spiritual heritage. I remember as a youth being ask to lead in prayer, read the Scripture, or share a devotion during family worship. These experiences provided the groundwork for my worship and ministry as an adult.

The key to family worship, especially when young children are involved, is to avoid being locked into anything rigid or formal. Families may want to select one night a week for a half an hour (less with very young children) for singing, prayer, sharing, and telling Bible stories. After sharing a lesson with my young children, I often assigned them parts and helped them act out the story. This allowed them to respond actively to the truth. It also served to reinforce the lesson I was teaching them.

A special treat like popcorn, roasted marsh mellows, or apple slices provides a "sweet conclusion" to family devotions. My children always looked forward to these very special times together. I worked hard to make the lessons fun and engaging so they would begin to value and appreciate the experience of worship.

Individual. God's worth may be appreciated in private as well. You may enjoy worshiping God in the quietness of a lofty mountain peak or on a grassy riverbank. You can worship in the privacy of your bedroom, den, or office. The importance of private worship is highlighted by J. B. Phillips: "If the Christian is to maintain the spiritual life within him, he must by desperate resolution elbow a space in his daily activities when he can obey the command to 'be still and know that I am God.'"

By commending individual or private worship, I am not advocating that you "worship" God on the golf course or ski slopes instead of gathering corporately for worship. The writer of Hebrews warns against neglecting our corporate gatherings for worship (Hebrews 10:25). Individual worship is a personal contemplation of God's worth which is designed to supplement—not replace—corporate and family worship.

The book that has helped me most in developing my private worship is the hymnal. As I read the great hymns of the faith, their lofty words, theology, and poetic expression raise my heart to God. I am often surprised by how quickly the minutes slip by as I spend time with God at worship.

Worthy Worship

Jesus rebuked the Scribes and Pharisees for honoring God with their lips while their hearts were far from Him (Mark 7:6-7). Their worship was in vain. We must learn to appreciate God in spirit and truth—not just with our lips, but with our total being. Such worship is the pathway to satisfaction and success in our spiritual lives.

Study and Review Questions

1. In your own words, tell what it means to worship God. Relate a unique or special worship experience you remember.
2. Jesus directs his followers to worship "in spirit and truth." What does this mean?
3. How important is it to have a theology of worship? Should the focus be on developing the theology or applying the truth?

4. Praise is the public acknowledgment of God's greatness and goodness. How have you praised God this week?

5. Writing a psalm testimony is an exciting way to prepare for praising God. Recall an incident in which God answered a prayer or intervened in a special way. Write a short "psalm of praise," focusing on God and what He has done for you.[22]

6. What are some innovative and creative ways God can be worshiped corporately? How can you encourage the implementation of these new forms of worship in your congregation?

7. Evaluate your individual and family worship. What steps might you take to enhance these worship opportunities?

8. Plan an outdoor worship experience for your family. You might combine this with a picnic at your favorite park or a hike along a wilderness trail. Consider how the outdoor setting might enhance your worship experience.

---

[22] For further instructions on writing your psalm, see my book *Your Psalm of Praise*, available on Amazon.com/books.

Chapter 11
THE SUCCESSFUL WOMAN

"An excellent wife is the crown of her husband, but she who shames him is as rottenness in his bones" (Proverbs 12:4). As the proverb indicates, a wife can be a man's greatest asset or his worst liability.

Katherine von Bora, a former nun, became the wife of Martin Luther. This godly woman was a wonderful wife and mother. Luther paid her the highest tribute when he said, "I would not exchange Katie for France or for Venice." He later remarked, "The highest gift and favor of God is a pious, kind, godly, and domestic wife, with whom you may live peaceably, and to whom you may entrust all your possessions, your body and your life." Katie Luther was a wise and successful woman, a crown to her husband.

John Wesley, the founder of Methodism, was not so fortunate as Luther. In his late forties he married a young widow, Mary Vazeille. This woman darkened thirty years of Wesley's life with intolerable jealousy, malicious gossip, and violent outbursts of temper. She would open her husband's letters, seize his papers, and humiliate him publicly. One cannot but wonder if Wesley's itinerant ministry on horseback was not, in part, a way of escape from an unpleasant home life.

Mary Wesley finally left her husband. In a letter to his estranged wife, Wesley told Mary that if she lived to be a thousand years old, she could not undo the mischief she had caused. Mary Wesley was anything but a crown to her husband. She was a cross and a curse.

No doubt, we all want to be successful in our marriages, ministries, and careers. How can women be more like a Katie Luther and less like a Mary Wesley? The answer can be found in the description of the worthy woman of Proverbs 31.

The woman of Proverbs 31 is married and has a family. Yet she can be a model for single women as well. The real focus of this passage is on the character qualities of the godly woman. The activities of a single woman may differ, but the principles of this passage are applicable to both the married and the single.

Many women today are intimidated and discouraged when they read Proverbs 31. "How can any woman," they ask, "attain this high standard of excellence?" It is not the intent of Scripture to bring discouragement by presenting this text. While many view this biblical "Wonder Woman" as an *ideal* to emulate, not an absolute *standard* by which all women should be measured, I think there is a better interpretation of this text. I suggest that Proverbs 31 provides a *composite picture* of the kinds of activities and accomplishments a woman can attain over a lifetime. While every woman is gifted differently, all can grow and develop through the encouragement and support of a loving husband.

For women who seek success in their marriage and family life, the woman of Proverbs 31 provides broad perimeters for her spiritual growth, family ministry, and personal career. As we explore her life and character, we will discover what made her so successful.

Her Spiritual Life

First in importance for any successful woman must be her spiritual and devotional life. The woman of Proverbs 31 made her spiritual life a sacred priority. "Charm is deceitful and beauty is vain, but a woman who fears the LORD, she shall be praised" (31:30). As we discovered earlier, the "fear of the Lord" is a reverent respect for God that is manifested by love, obedience, and service. The one who truly "fears the Lord" delights in the observance of His commandments (Psalm 112:1).

Making her spiritual life a sacred priority does not imply that a godly woman should neglect her physical wellbeing. On the contrary, the believer's body is the very temple of God (2 Corinthians 6:16), and should glorify Him by being as fit, well dressed, and attractive as possible. A Christian woman is an ambassador for Jesus, representing Him to the unbelieving world. She will want to present herself in an attractive and pleasing manner *for the Lord*.

138

Yet there must be a balance. All too often the emphasis is on the physical, while spiritual qualities are neglected. We must not lose the divine perspective. "For God sees not as man sees, for man looks at the outward appearance, but the LORD looks at the heart" (1 Samuel 16:7). Since it is the spiritual aspect of the person that endures, godly women must give this area top priority (1 Peter 3:3-4).

A woman with a spiritually minded husband must beware of depending upon his spiritual life to sustain her. The husband who takes an active role as a spiritual leader in the home will initiate regular times of prayer and Bible study with his wife. But if those special times are the extent of a wife's devotional life, she is in danger of becoming spiritually disabled.

Hannah, the mother of Samuel, is a fine example of a woman who made her spiritual life a sacred priority. Her fervent prayer in the tabernacle suggests that she must have spent time in in prayer daily (1 Samuel 1:12-15). She knew God well enough to "pour out" her soul before Him. Hannah was also a woman of the Word. Her thorough knowledge of Scripture is evidenced by the many allusions to God's attributes and actions in the praise she offers at Shiloh (1 Samuel 2:1-10).

Early in my marriage, I realized that my wife's busy schedule as a new grade school teacher hindered the development of her personal devotional life. After making breakfast and cleaning up the kitchen, she would hurry off to her duties as a second-grade teacher. One day I suggested that I wash the breakfast dishes, giving her ten minutes in the morning for prayer and Bible study. This was a significant step in Nancy's spiritual development. Over the years I have seen her relationship with God mature and strengthen. As she has matured spiritually, so Nancy has grown more beautiful in godly character and virtue. After forty-five years of marriage, I'm still washing breakfast dishes, and Nancy is still growing spiritually!

Think of the spiritual development that would take place if we gave as much time to our spiritual lives as we do to tennis, jogging, Facebook, or our smart phones! By making your spiritual life a sacred priority, you will realize your full potential and become the successful woman God has enabled you to be.

Her Personal Life

The godly woman of Proverbs 31 developed her personal life in a number of significant areas. Remember, she is a composite and illustrates the variety of opportunities available to women as part of their personal lives and careers. It is possible that she took classes at Jerusalem Community College. More likely, she learned these skills from a loving mother who took child training seriously. As a result of her training and experience, she has become a skillful and resourceful person. Consider her abilities:

Weaving (v. 13). "She looks for wool and flax, and works with her hands in delight."

Gourmet cooking (v. 14). "She is like merchant ships; she brings her food from afar."

Investing (v. 16). "She considers a field and buys it."

Gardening (v. 16). "From her earnings she plants a vineyard."

Exercising (v. 17). "She girds herself with strength, and makes her arms strong."

Sewing (v. 22). "She makes coverings for herself; her clothing is fine linen and purple."

So talented is she as a seamstress that she is able to sell clothes and belts to provide additional income for her household (31:24). As a result of developing her personal life, this woman is poised and confident. We are told, "Strength and dignity are her clothing, and she smiles at the future" (31:25).

140

Married women with family responsibilities sometimes look with envy upon women with careers outside the home. They long for the stimulation, challenge, and excitement of being out in the world, involved with people, and acquiring new abilities. Not every woman, however, needs outside employment to attain these goals. Many women are able to develop their personal lives at home where they can also care for their family responsibilities.

A wife and mother need not settle for a life of doing dishes and changing diapers, as important as these tasks are. A wife may want to take a class in gourmet cooking to develop her skills as a hostess. Or perhaps she enjoys crafts and has found that selling her creations is a nice source of extra income. A wife who enjoys writing may want to attend a seminar to refine her skills as a free-lance writer. The sky is the limit!

For the woman who desires to develop her personal life, there are many exciting challenges. Each day offers new opportunities to learn, grow, and mature. Such a woman can be poised and confident, because she is attaining the potential God has for her.

Her Family Life

According to Solomon, the wise married woman "builds her house" (Proverbs 14:1). Having recognized the priority of developing her own spiritual and personal life, she fulfills her family responsibilities by ministering to her husband and children.

Paul pointed out that the single life is a valid option for a woman to consider. In fact, he preferred this option in view of the greater opportunities the single life affords in serving others (1 Corinthians 7:32-35). Over the years I have had a number of godly, single women in my classes. I like to encourage them with a quote from a friend and colleague who teaches Hebrew at Denver Seminary. On her sixtieth birthday as a single lady, Dr. Helen Dallaire posted on her Facebook page, "Following God and serving Him wholeheartedly is what the life of a Christian should be about, whether one is single or married. Contentment does not come from your marital status; it comes from the Lord. *To single people out there, serve God with every fiber of your being and He will take care of your marital status."*

And yet, in the biblical period, most women married and had a family. And so Scripture addresses the matter of a woman's family life.

A Suitable Helper. In relationship to her husband, the woman has the role of a "suitable helper." In Genesis 2:18 God declared, "It is not good for the man to be alone; I will make him a helper suitable for him." Woman was designed by God to be a man's helpmate—literally, "a helper agreeing to him."

Woman is man's mental, physical, and spiritual counterpart. The word *helper* does not suggest inferiority, for it is used in the Hebrew Bible of God Himself (Psalm 33:20; 146:5). Woman was divinely designed to share with man in all the activities of life including exercising dominion, raising children, and worshiping God. In relationship to her husband woman is "a fellow heir of the grace of life" (1 Peter 3:7).

The successful woman of Proverbs 31 seeks the best for her husband. "She does him good and not evil all the days of her life" (31:12). Several other proverbs give suggestions as to how she may accomplish this. *First*, she shouldn't be a destructive critic of her husband (Proverbs 12:4). He will have plenty of critics without her. Instead, a wife should be on the lookout for opportunities to commend her husband for his work or ministry. *Second*, she must learn to live within the family's budget (19:14). By making prudent use of her grocery money, the family can have more to enjoy together. *Third*, she ought to manifest a sweet and supportive spirit, creating an atmosphere which will make home like a bit of heaven on earth (21:9).

A good wife gives her husband reason to have confidence in her. "The heart of her husband trusts in her, and he will have no lack of gain" (31:11). A wife's exemplary conduct will enable her husband to trust her in all family matters—spiritual, moral, social, financial, and medical. A husband should be able to endorse his paycheck, turn it over to his wife, and have perfect confidence that the financial responsibilities entrusted to her will be cared for.

Someone has said, "To be trusted is even a greater compliment than to be loved." A kind and prudent wife will enjoy being both.

A Devoted Mother. The successful woman of Proverbs 31 made her maternal responsibilities a high priority. We are told, "She looks well to the ways of her household, and does not eat the bread of idleness" (Proverbs 31:27). Abraham Lincoln once wrote, "All that I am or hope to be I owe to my angel mother." Mothers are the potters God uses to shape and influence the pliable lives of their young children. What specifically does the woman of Proverbs 31 do for her children?

First, she feeds them. "She rises also while it is still night, and gives food to her household" (31:15). I have fond memories of my mother serving me a steaming plate of grits and eggs before I hurried off to school or work. A good mother does not lie in bed while her children forage about in the kitchen for breakfast. She is diligent to prepare healthy and nutritional meals for her children.

Second, she works hard in the home doing her household chores. So diligent is she that "her lamp does not go out at night' (31:18). A devoted mother doesn't work regular hours; she works *all* hours. She doesn't just have an eight-to-five job that ends at punch-out time. She often must work into the night folding laundry, baking cookies, and packing lunches.

Third, she makes sure that her children are well clothed. "She is not afraid of the snow for her household, for all her household are clothed with scarlet" (31:21). A mother need not be a seamstress to be a good provider of clothes for her family. She should make sure that her children have shoes that fit and clothes that are clean and warm.

Fourth, she teaches her children. "She opens her mouth in wisdom, and the teaching of kindness is on her tongue"

(31:26). In Proverbs the father and mother are placed on exactly the same footing as teachers of their children (1:8; 4:3; 6:20; 31:1). In the biblical period parents "together shared the responsibility for the education of the child."[23] The late Dr. Frank Gaebelein once commented that "the home is still the greatest educational force."[24]

Mothers have the tremendous opportunity of teaching their young children not only practical skills but truth about God and principles of morality. A wise and successful mother will take an active part in the education of her children. She won't leave this important matter solely to the professionals. She will seek to enhance, supplement, and sometimes correct the formal education her child receives.

A London editor submitted a list of the Prime Minister's former teachers to Winston Churchill. The list was returned with this comment. "You have omitted to mention the greatest of my teachers—my mother."

A wise mother will read to her children as often as possible, take them to the library regularly, and plan creative educational activities like letter-writing and craft projects. Like Eunice, the mother of Timothy (2 Timothy 1:5; 3:15), the wise woman will make a strong impact on the education and spiritual development of her children.

Being a suitable helper and a devoted mother is one of the greatest challenges women will ever face. None would claim that their task is easy. It takes lots of hard work. But by God's grace, it is possible to be all that they want to be in relationship to their family.

Her Ministry

While the woman of Proverbs 31 is involved in a cottage industry and various other enterprises, her family is quite clearly the focus of her ministry.

---

[23] N.R. Whybray, *Wisdom in Proverbs* (Naperville, Ill.: A.R. Allenson, 1965), p. 42.

[24] Frank E. Gaebelein, "The Bible: Both the Source and the Setting for Learning," *Christianity Today* (February 6, 1981), p. 20.

We live in an era when over sixty percent of women in America work outside the home. Three reasons are usually cited for the increased number of working women: (1) more single parent mothers (2) economic challenges of living on one income (3) personal desire for a career. Research suggests that the third group is the biggest reason why mothers enter the work force.

Although not all my friends agree on this subject, I believe that a woman with children—especially young children—should avoid taking a job outside the home. Now, I realize that the economic circumstances of some women, especially widows and divorced mothers, may require that they seek outside employment. But I am suggesting that this ought to be the exception rather than the norm.

But before someone "writes me off" as a relic of a bygone era, consider the advantages of a mother giving her primary attention to her family rather than the demands of a job.

First, a career mother is able to give her energy and attention to the primary responsibility God has placed before her. Mothers who spend the day pursuing a career outside the home have at least eight hours less per day to devote to their family. Responsibility for the daily care of the children must be delegated to someone else. When the working mother comes home, weary from a long day at her workplace, she has little energy for her children or her home. Some mothers seem to manage this fairly well, but eventually something has to give. And often it is time with the children.

Second, a career mother can be more effective in her ministry to her church and community. Working mothers must limit their opportunities for personal ministry. They have little time for taking an elderly widow shopping, preparing meals for a sick mother, or leading a women's Bible study. Many working women must excuse themselves from church and community service because of the time commitment required by an eight-hour-a-day job.

Third, a career mother is unable to provide adult supervision for her children after school. In 1980, 52% of mothers worked outside the home. According to the 2010 census, 67% of mothers are in the workforce. The Department of Labor estimates that 32 million children have mothers who work outside the home, and 13 million of these children are under the age of 14. According to a report by the Pew Research Center, working mothers report feeling stressed about balancing work and family. When asked in general how they feel about their time, 40% of working moms said they always feel rushed. This compares with 24% of the general public and 26% of stay-at-home moms.[25] While some mothers can arrange their work to be home after school, many cannot. Many of these "latchkey" children spend three hours a day watching TV and fiddling around the house without adult supervision.

My purpose here is not to lay a guilt trip on those mothers who find it necessary to work outside the home. But I would like to challenge those who do so merely because of personal desire to consider the alternatives.

Any woman who seeks the fulfillment, excitement, and prestige that a career offers should consider the possibility of working at home. Dr. Dobson's radio ministry, "Focus on the Family," published a booklet entitled, "Working at Home: Ways to Supplement Family Income." It presents twenty-five ways to earn extra income under your own roof, from custom typing to running an answering service. Perhaps a creative alternative to a secular career may provide the balance women may be seeking between family responsibility and career objectives.

Paul encouraged the older women to train the younger women (those with young families) to be "workers at home" (Titus 2:3-5). The biblical pattern is for women with children to make their family the focus of their work and ministry. This is clearly the priority of the successful woman of

---

[25]Kim Parker, "Women, Work, and Motherhood," A Sampler of Recent Pew Research Findings (April 13, 2012), www.PewSocialTrends.org.

Proverbs 31, who "looks well to the ways of her household" (31:27).

A Worthy Woman

I noticed an article in a ladies' magazine which told the story of a young woman whose work as a lawyer led to her becoming a state administrative judge. Her marriage was the casualty of her career. She divorced her husband because "he demanded so much from me that I couldn't meet those demands and practice law at the same time." She told the magazine interviewer, "His stuff always came first."

The most influential person in my life was a woman. She was a bright, talented lady capable in the areas of finance, administration, teaching, and counseling. She gave over sixty years of her life to her career as a homemaker. She raised five children—a seminary professor, an attorney, a school-teacher, a businessman, and a son who is now in heaven. She has been a model for me throughout my life. When I was stricken with polio, this godly woman prayed for me throughout that first painful and uncertain night. I am what I am today because of *my mother.*

Did my mom miss out on fulfillment in life by not pursuing a career? I suspect that she found as much satisfaction and sense of accomplishment in being a homemaker as the most lucrative career could offer.

It is in the home that a married woman has the greatest potential for success and the greatest danger of failure. I am thankful for wives and mothers who devote their primary focus on their families. May their children and husbands rise up and bless them, saying, "Many daughters have done nobly, but you excel them all" (Proverbs 31:29).

Study and Review Questions
1. Does Proverbs 31:10-31 set forth a standard for all women to meet? How would you explain this text to a young wife or mother?

2. What is the key to the success of the woman of Proverbs 31?
3. Why is the spiritual life of a woman such a high priority?
4. The wise woman of Proverbs 31 shows a concern for developing her personal life. What areas of your own personal life would you like to develop?
5. What does it mean for a wife to be a "suitable helper" (Genesis 2:18)? Does this term suggest inferiority? Why not?
6. The woman of Proverbs 31 has a ministry that extends beyond her family (31:20). What opportunities of ministry beyond your family might you pursue?
7. What scriptural principles might guide you in a decision whether or not to pursue a career outside your home?

Chapter 12
THE SUCCESSFUL MAN

Eric Liddell, whose life was dramatized in the movie *Chariots of Fire*, was the son of a Scottish Presbyterian missionary couple. He was born in China during the convulsive years of the Boxer Revolution. When he was five years old, his parents were given a furlough and he visited Scotland for the first time. When his parents returned to China to continue their work, arrangements were made for Eric and his older brother Rob to attend a boarding school for missionary children in London.

Eric later attended Eltham College where he excelled at athletics, particularly as a sprinter. His record at Eltham of 10.2 seconds in the 100-yard dash still stands unbroken. Eric continued his running career when he entered the University of Edinburgh in the autumn of 1920. He trained regularly, but not excessively. Soon he was winning races all over Scotland. As a result of his outstanding performance at the AAA Championships at Stamford Bridge in London, Liddell was selected to represent Great Britain in the 1924 Olympic Games in Paris.

When the time tables for the races came out, Eric discovered that the 100-meter heats were scheduled on a Sunday. "I'm not running," he said. Reverence for the Lord's Day was a principle Liddell would not compromise—even to compete in the Olympic Games. Criticism by the press and public jibes could not cause him to change his mind. Not even the Prince of Wales could persuade him to run the race "for the sake of his country."

Withdrawing from the 100-meter race, Liddell was given a place in the 400. Although not viewed as a serious contender, Eric Liddell captured the hearts of the British people by winning a gold medal. His time in the 400-meter race of 47.6 seconds set a new world record.

That is the story of Eric Liddell that many people are familiar with. What most people don't know is that a year later, Scotland's greatest athlete stepped from the public arena to return to China with the London Missionary

Society. On February 21, 1945, after a twenty-year ministry in China, the powerful runner lay dying in a Japanese internment camp, his energy sapped away by privation and malnutrition. After an attack of influenza and what was thought to be a stroke, the "flying Scotsman" was dead.[26]

Eric Liddell, a man to be admired and remembered, was not a great leader or an inspired thinker. He was simply a man of convictions, one who knew what he ought to do—and did it.

Eric Liddell was successful because he knew God, believed God, and obeyed God. He was the kind of person *you* can be. The world is looking desperately for such men today.

His Character

A familiar advertisement reads, "The Marines are looking for a few good men." The point is subtle but clear. The Marines say they are interested in quality, not quantity.

God is looking for a few good men too. Throughout history it has been the "few good men" who have made the difference—the two spies who believed Israel could conquer the land of Canaan, the three hundred warriors who marched with Gideon, and the eleven disciples who spread the gospel throughout the known world.

One quality of such men is mentioned in the Psalms: "How blessed is the man who fears the LORD, who greatly delights in His commandments" (112:1). As we have learned, the "fear of the Lord" is virtually equivalent to knowing God and appreciating His awesome reputation. The one who truly fears Him will show it not by trembling during prayers, but by obeying His commandments.

The one who fears God "delights" or "takes pleasure in His commandments (Psalm 1:2). For the wise and successful man, the teachings of God's Word are not an irksome burden but a source of joy and encouragement. Delighting in God's law means knowing God's teachings

---

[26] For a full biography of Eric Liddell, see Sally Magnusson's *The Flying Scotsman* (New York: Quartet Books, 1981).

and happily obeying them. This is the way to righteousness, life, and prosperity (Deuteronomy 30:15-20).

The psalmist exclaims, "Oh how I love Your law!" (Psalm 119:97). Such a love for God's Word is "caught" rather than "taught." It comes from consistently reading and applying the Scriptures to one's life.

During my years of study, God's Word has become like a devoted companion and friend, a source of challenge, encouragement, and sometimes rebuke. The words of Scripture express the joy in my heart when I am happy. There I find consolation when my heart is troubled. Abraham Lincoln once said, "I believe the Bible is the best gift that God has ever given to man. All the good from the Savior of the world is communicated to us through this Book."

Psalm 15 contains a detailed list of the characteristics of the wise and successful man. He is righteous, truthful, respectful, considerate, morally discriminating, trustworthy, and does not take advantage of others (15:2-5). The psalmist concludes with an encouraging promise: "He who does all these things will never be shaken." This man is as stable and enduring as the Rock of Gibraltar because he knows and obeys God.

His Blessings

The man who truly fears God delights in His teachings (Psalm 112). Verses 2 through 5 should not be taken as a personal guarantee but rather as a general description of the kinds of blessings that result from following God's wisdom.

Happy Children. The first blessing mentioned is about family life. It is said of the wise man, "His descendants will be mighty on the earth; the generation of the upright will be blessed" (v. 2). The word *mighty* normally means physically strong or heroic in battle. Here it is used metaphorically to describe the wise man's offspring as influential and respected. His descendants are described as "upright." They follow in the footsteps of their wise father and consequently enjoy the same blessings. It is remarkable what a source of positive influence and blessing a godly father can be for his children.

Material Provision. Verse 3 contains a general principle that may have exceptions in our fallen world today. It is said of the man who fears the Lord, "Wealth and riches are in his house, and his righteousness endures forever." Generally speaking, the righteous man who follows God's guidelines in business and ethics will prosper. This statement does not promote the "prosperity gospel" by suggesting that everyone who follows these precepts will be become a millionaire. But it is true that if a man follows God's wisdom and avoids financial entanglements, he will generally be better off than the man who doesn't (Psalm 34:10; 84:11).

Divine Guidance. The psalmist declared, "Light arises in the darkness for the upright; he is gracious and compassionate and righteous" (v. 4). "Light" and "darkness" here are being used metaphorically. In the Old Testament, light is associated with life, salvation, prosperity, wisdom, and justice. Darkness is associated with death, failure, suffering, folly and sin. God's commandments are said to be a "light" and a "lamp" (Proverbs 6:23; Psalm 119:105). The psalmist declared, "The unfolding of Your words give light; it gives understanding to the simple (Psalm 119:130).

Light refers to guidance or direction in Psalm 112:4. The wise man is blessed with the light of God's Word that will penetrate the dark shadows life's difficulties. Isaiah looked prophetically to the coming of the Messiah as a great Light shining in a land of deep darkness (9:2). Jesus claimed to be the "light of the world" (John 8:12, 9:5), and those who are wise will walk by His light.

On May 21, 1941, the "unsinkable" Nazi battleship, the Bismark, was sighted in the north Atlantic. Immediately, planes and ships from the Royal British Navy sped to the scene. As the Bismark headed toward the German-controlled French coast, the massive battleship suddenly swung around and reentered the area where the British ships were massed in greatest strength. At the same time, the Bismark began to steer an erratic zigzag course. A torpedo had damaged her rudder. Without the ability to steer a course to safety, the "unsinkable" Bismark was sunk!

For God's people, the "rudder" is the Word of God. Without its guidance, we are as vulnerable to attack by the world and the Devil as the crippled Bismark was to the British Navy.

Fair Dealings. The successful man of Psalm 112 is ready to extend a helping hand to those in need. "It is well with the man who is gracious and lends; He will maintain his cause in judgment" (v. 5). The "lending" referred to here is not a business transaction but an act of charity. The one who is kind to others will experience fair dealings when he himself is on trial or subject to critical examination. In the midst of such uncertain circumstances, the wise man will stand firm because he is rightly related to both God and people.

His Success

Wisdom is the practical and successful application of God's truth to life's experiences. The wise man will get the best out of life by choosing the way of prosperity over the way of adversity. Though he may experience temporary setbacks, he knows that the ultimate outcome will be victory. According to Scripture, wisdom results in success (Ecclesiastes 10:10).

Stability. The first evidence of success in the life of the wise man is his stability. "For he will never be shaken" (Psalm 112:6). The word shaken literally means, "made to stumble." The righteous man has that certain steadfastness which all men long for. This steadfastness rests solidly on his relationship with God and his application of God's truth. The wise man is confident in God as well as his own abilities, even in times of difficulty. He is one on who others can relay when the going gets tough.

Honor. The psalmist declared, "The righteous will be remembered forever" (112:6). The reason is suggested in Psalm 111:4. God's words are said to be a memorial. The good deeds of a righteous man will be an enduring memorial of his life.[27] In Proverbs we read, "The reward of humility and the fear of the LORD are riches, honor and life" (22:4). By his consistent practice of doing good the wise man will gain recognition and honor. According to the Jewish Talmud, "There is no need to set up monuments to the righteous; their acts are their memorial."[28]

Confidence. The psalmist declared, "He will not fear evil tidings; his heart is steadfast, trusting in the LORD." (112:7). The wise man is not exempt from unfortunate circumstances or temporary setbacks, but he is able to face them with confidence. He does not live with continual fear or apprehension because he has absolute confidence in God.

In the Hebrew Bible the word "heart" is used most often in the metaphorical sense to refer to a person's inner or immaterial nature. Wisdom and understanding are seated in the heart (Proverbs 16:23). In this sense, the "heart" is virtually a synonym for the mind. One whose "heart is steadfast" isn't double-minded, doubtful, or fickle. That person possesses inner conviction, confidence and certainty. He takes the bad news along with the good, knowing that God is accomplishing His sovereign purposes.

---

[27] A. Cohen, *The Psalms: Soncino Books of the Bible* (London: The Soncino Press, 1945), p. 377.

[28] H. C. Leupold, *Exposition of the Psalms* (Grand Rapids: Baker Book House, 1959), p. 789.

Victory. The psalmist said, "His heart is upheld, he will not fear, until he looks with satisfaction on his adversaries" (112:8). Because of the steadfastness of his inner person, the wise man has nothing to fear—even in the face of opposition.

Such fearlessness is an important quality, for the wise man is sure to be opposed. No man can serve God without encountering the forces of evil. But the wise man is confident that by God's grace he will eventually see victory. Yet he won't gloat over his victory. The words "with satisfaction" are not in the Hebrew text. The phrase in the original, "looks on his adversaries," is a metaphorical expression and suggests the idea of "witnessing the enemies defeat." The ultimate victory of the godly man is highlighted elsewhere: "For whatever is born of God overcomes the world; and this is the victory that has overcome the world—our faith" (1 John 5:4).

The success of the righteous man is described: "And he will be like a tree firmly planted by streams of water, which yields its fruit in its season, and its leaf does not wither; and in whatever he does, he prospers" (Psalm 1:3).

The righteous man is like that deeply rooted three that receives its nourishment from a steadily flowing underground stream, not the uncertain rains. His life produces fruit and his undertakings ultimately succeed. Opposition and the buffeting of life's circumstances fail to turn him from his purpose or overcome his resolve.

On October 12, 1962, the Pacific Northwest was buffeted by the hurricane force winds of the Columbus Day Storm. In Eugene, Oregon, the high winds lifted the roof off Roosevelt Junior High and deposited it in bits and pieces over a distance of several city blocks. Many of the stately Douglas fir trees on the University of Oregon campus were blown down. Upon observing the trees toppled by the high winds, it was discovered that they had shallow roots. They were not deep enough to sustain the trees under such buffeting.

The wise man sinks his roots deep into the Word of God. Then, when he is confronted with the inevitable storms of life, he will stand fast.

His Opposite

The last two verses of Psalm 112 set forth a contrast between the wise man and the foolish man, the one who abides by God's standards and the one who does not. Of the wise man it is said, "He has given freely to the poor; his righteousness endures forever; his horn will be exalted in honor" (v. 9). His generous acts of charity will leave a lasting impression on others. His kindness will not soon be forgotten (Proverbs 22:9).

The word *horn* is used in Scripture as a metaphor of strength since it is the focus of a bull's power (Zechariah 1:19-21; Daniel 8:20-21). To have one's horn exalted or raised up in honor is to receive public recognition or acclaim for one's accomplishments. God is the one who does this. "And all the horns of the wicked He will cut off, but the horns of the righteous will be lifted up" (Psalm 75:10).

The description of the wicked man is set in obvious contrast with the verse: "The wicked will see it and be vexed; he will gnash his teeth and melt away; the desire of the wicked will perish" (112:10). The context indicates that the wicked man will see the prosperity and success of the righteous and be bitterly provoked. While the righteous sees the downfall of the wicked (v. 8), the wicked will witness the vindication of the upright. Now the tables have turned. The wicked gnashes his teeth in anger and frustration. He "melts" away like a piece of ice on hot pavement. His goals and ambitions won't be realized. His evil desires and purposes will perish with him.

We must acknowledge with Leupold that "this is not revengeful and unkind thinking in regard to the wicked. It is insight into how the Lord rewards those that truly fear him and prevents the enemies of His people from seeing their evil purposes come to fruition. That is something for which God may be truly praised."[29]

Jimmy Hoffa became president of the Teamsters' union when the incumbent went to prison, accused of stealing union funds. Unfortunately, Hoffa followed in the footsteps of his predecessor. In 1964, Hoffa was sentenced to a total of thirteen years in prison for fraudulent use of the union pension fund and tampering with a jury. His sentence was commuted in 1971 on the condition that he not engage in union affairs until 1980.

On July 30, 1975, Jimmy Hoffa disappeared from a suburban Detroit restaurant. He was presumably murdered. It is reported that he was seeking to regain his position in the Teamsters' union when he disappeared. Seven years and four months later, the once powerful Jimmy Hoffa was declared legally dead.

Jimmy Hoffa's life well illustrates the kind of man Psalm 112:10 describes. Hoffa was ambitious, clever, and imposing. But he was not wise. His unethical dealings brought about his eventual demise. Since his body was never found, there is not even a grave to stand as mute testimony to his former existence.

Your Decision

In the conclusion of His Sermon on the Mount, Jesus stood in the tradition of Israel's sages, contrasting the wise man who built his house on a rock with the foolish man who built on sand (Matthew 7:24-27). When the rain, wind, and floods came, the house built on the solid foundation stood firm. But the house build on sand was utterly destroyed.

Jesus used this simple story to emphasize the importance of responding to His teaching. The wise man hears Jesus' teachings and acts upon them. The foolish man hears, but does not heed.

---

[29] H. C. Leupold, *Exposition of the Psalms* (Grand Rapids: Baiker Book House, 1959), p. 789.

We are faced with a decision—to be forgetful hearers or effectual doers (James 1:25). The choice we make will determine our destiny. Those who respond to the teachings of Scripture have a happy and secure future despite the inevitable storms of life. Those who hear and *disregard* God's words of wisdom ensure their own destruction.

Eric Liddell made his decision early in life to heed the wise counsel of God's Word. He once said, "Obedience to God's will is the secret of spiritual knowledge and insight. It is not willingness to know, but to do God's will that brings enlightenment and certainty."[30]

It's really up to us. The success Eric Liddell achieved is not the exclusive possession of a privileged few. We can choose to be successful too.

Study Questions

1. Why is the world attracted to such a person as Eric Liddell? What qualities in his life are attractive even to those who don't know God personally?
2. Explain the meaning of the expression, "the fear of the Lord." How does the second line of Psalm 112:1 illuminate this expression?
3. According to Psalm 112:2-5. What blessings will the wise man enjoy?
4. Psalm 112:6 illustrates the kind of success the wise man can expect to enjoy. How does his success differ from that which the world seeks? In what ways it is similar?
5. Compare the destiny of the wise and righteous man with that of the wicked as outlined in Psalm 112:9-10.
6. Have you made a decision to pursue the path of success? If so, how has your decision been evidenced in your life? What steps can you take to continue living in this manner?

---

[30] "The Muscular Christianity of Eric Liddell," *Christianity Today* (June 14, 1985), p. 23.

Conclusion:
UNLOCKING YOUR FUTURE

William Graham Scroggie was a man of the Word. Born in 1877, the son of a Scottish evangelist, Scroggie entered Spurgeon's College in London at the age of nineteen to prepare for the ministry. As a result of his opposition to theological liberalism and worldliness, he had the humiliating experience of being turned out of his first and second pastorates. It didn't appear that Scroggie was headed for a very successful career.

Trusting the Lord to provide for his financial needs, Scroggie devoted the next two years to personal study of the Scriptures. He worked his way through the Bible, outlining the books, developing his theology, and gaining an understanding of the major themes of Scripture. These studies laid the foundation for his future ministry of preaching and writing.

Scroggie's next two pastorates were lengthy and fruitful. His expositions of Scripture drew large audiences at Charlotte Chapel in Edinburgh. In 1938, after two years of itinerant preaching on several continents, Scroggie was called to pastor Spurgeon's Metropolitan Tabernacle in London where he enjoyed six years of fruitful ministry. He retired in 1944 to devote the rest of his life to his writing ministry. During these years Scroggie authored numerous books, including works on the Psalms and the Gospels.

William Scroggie was a man who focused on the Bible. He was convinced that God's Word must have an important place in the lives of God's people. This concern is highlighted in the preface of his last book. There Scroggie asserts that Christians must know the Bible better than any other book. Then he adds, "The Bible is given to us that we might know God, and live the life of His plan for us."[31]

---

[31] W. Graham Scroggie, *The Unfolding Drama of Redemption* (Grand Rapids: Zondervan Publishing House, 1972), p. 17.

It was a commitment to knowing God and obeying His Word that enabled Scroggie to achieve success in his life and ministry. It is encouraging to know that what took place in his life of not just an unusual exception but rather the norm for people who have discovered God's key to success.

God's Key to Success

We have covered a lot of terrain in our search for success. We began in Ecclesiastes 10:10 where we discovered that "wisdom has the advantage of giving success." The search for success must begin at Wisdom's door. And Wisdom's first and foremost lesson is "the fear of the Lord" (Proverbs 9:10), which we have learned is simply knowing God and obeying His Word.

Wisdom is God's key to success. But we must define success God's way. Being successful does not mean that we won't have any problems. It does mean that we will be better prepared to handle the difficulties in life we all encounter. Among other things, wise people will avoid the devastating results of sin, the burdens of financial entanglements, the sorrows of marital failure, discontent in circumstances over which they have no control, and the reproach of immorality. This is the kind of success that all God's people can enjoy.

Success begins with knowing God. As you have studied this book, you have probably reflected on your own relationship with God. One's knowledge of God is not limited to a recital of His attributes. According to the Bible, there is only one way to get to know God. Jesus said, "I and the Father are one" (John 10:30). Later he declared, "He who has seen Me has seen the Father" (John 14:9). Jesus told Thomas, "I am the way, the truth, and the life; no one comes to the Father but through Me" (John 14:6).

Success takes place as we know and obey God. The Word of God is our guide to living life as the Creator planned it. The Bible serves as a handbook on the art of successful living. On the eve of the conquest of Canaan, God instructed Joshua to obey the law He had given, "so

160

that you may have success wherever you go" (Joshua 1:7). Through our study of the Bible we can grow in our knowledge of God and discover His good and perfect will for us.

God has set before each one of us the way of life and prosperity and the way of death and adversity. The pathway to success and prosperity is marked by the directives of God's Word. A neglect of these guidelines for life will result in avoidable casualties, unnecessary difficulties, and ultimate failure. The exhortation of Moses is applicable for us today: "Choose life in order that you may live, you and your descendants, by loving the LORD your God, by obeying His voice, and by holding fast to Him" (Deuteronomy 30:19-20).

Dealing with Past Failure

Few of us can look back on our lives without seeing the debris of moral, financial, ethical, or marital failure. The failure may reflect a situation in our lives before we came to know the One who came to save us from sin and sin's consequences. It may reflect a time when we lacked commitment and maturity, when the Deceiver had sway and we disregarded the "way of escape" (1 Corinthians 10:13).

God does not want us to wallow in the guilt of past failure. His desire is that we confess our failings and put them behind us. There is no need to dredge up the sins God has cast into the deepest sea (Micah 7:19).

John Mark, a young follower of Jesus, began as a failure. We don't know all the details, but for some reason he turned back on his first mission with Paul and Barnabas. This was apparently a great disappointment for Paul, and when the next mission was being planned, Paul refused to include John Mark (Acts 13:13, 15:38). John Mark really blew it! He was a failure.

Yet God gave this young man another chance. John Mark was invited to accompany Barnabas on a mission to Cyprus. Mark later served with Peter in Rome and, according to Eusebius, he recorded the preaching of Peter in what we know today as the Gospel of Mark.[32] Early Christian tradition records that Mark went on to found a church in Alexandria and became its first bishop. On the eve of his death, Paul wrote Timothy from his prison cell in Rome requesting that John Mark be brought to him. The apostle offered a brief word of explanation: "For he is useful to me for service" (2 Timothy 4:11). The man whom Paul had rejected for ministry had, in the end, proven himself "useful."

Mark's early failure in life did not destroy his potential for success as a minister of the gospel. He went on to accomplish great things for God. And if becoming a valued co-worker with Paul is not success, I don't know what is.

God delights in turning "failures" into success stories—to His honor and glory.

Coping with Success

Can you believe it? Success has its hazards. The danger that comes from being successful is that we begin to trust in ourselves—our own abilities, position of influence, and resources, rather than God's. This has happened again and again.

It happened to Uzziah, king of Judah, who enjoyed great success and was exalted to a position of prominence. We read, "But when he became strong, his heart was so proud that he acted corruptly, and he was unfaithful to the LORD his God" (2 Chronicles 26:16). As a result, God had to discipline the king. He lived out his days as a leper.

It happened to Nebuchadnezzar, ruler of the Babylonian Empire, who achieved great military success and was privileged to rebuild and beautify the lovely city of Babylon. Yet he too succumbed to pride. Gazing up that magnificent walled city, Nebuchadnezzar said, "Is this not Babylon the great, which I myself have built as a royal residence by the might of my power and for the glory of my majesty?"

---

[32] Eusebius, *Historia Ecclesiastica* 2.15.

(Daniel 4:30). God judged Nebuchadnezzar and his mind was changed to that of a beast, and for seven years he ate grass like an ox.

It happened to Jerusalem. God exalted the city above all others as a place of worship and seat of royalty. Jerusalem enjoyed a lovely setting, strong defenses, and the privileges of international trade. The city prospered and its fame was spread abroad. But then came pride. As the Prophet Ezekiel declared, "But you trusted in your beauty" (Ezekiel 16:15). Proverbs 16:18 teaches, "Pride goes before destruction, and a haughty spirit before stumbling." Such was the experience of the people of Jerusalem. Their exile to Babylon was God's judgment on prideful and disobedient Jerusalem.

John the Baptizer was different. He was called by God to serve as the Messiah's forerunner, introducing Jesus to the Jewish people of first-century. He did his task well, preaching repentance and announcing that Israel's prophesied kingdom was about to be established by Jesus. The response to his ministry was positive. People from Jerusalem, Judea, and Perea were going out to hear him preach the good news of the coming kingdom (Matthew 3:5-6).

But a day came when John's disciples began to leave him in order to follow Jesus. The crowds coming to hear John's preaching diminished while the multitudes following Jesus increased. It was a situation ripe for temptation to jealousy.

Yet, John knew that his task was to introduce people to the Messiah, to exalt the Lord. God gave John success in his ministry knowing that He would get the glory. John sought none of the glory for himself. In the face of temptation to be jealous of Jesus' growing ministry, John declared, "He must increase, but I must decrease" (John 3:30). Because of this humble and submissive attitude, Jesus was able to declare, "Among those born of women there has not arisen anyone greater than John the Baptizer" (Matthew 11:11).

In an interview, Professor Howard Hendricks offered some sage advice for the graduates of Dallas Seminary. In response to the question, "Do you have any words of wisdom for our graduates?" Hendricks wrote, "If I had to boil it down, I'd say 'Lie low and exalt grace,' because you can't promote yourself and Him at the same time. You are going to have to decide who is the center of attraction in your ministry."[33]

John the Baptizer grasped this crucial principle. He knew how to cope with success. He recognized that success ultimately came from God (John 3:27). He didn't allow it to go to his head. The Lord was able to entrust to John a generous measure of success in life because he knew that John would use it to glorify Him.

Eric Liddell experienced success, yet maintained humility. In his *Manual of Christian Discipleship*, he wrote, "Love recognizes that every gift and talent comes from God. It recognizes the responsibility to use and develop these gifts but not to become proud, arrogant, patronizing or to give itself airs because of them."[34]

In some measure, the degree of success God is willing to allow in our lives depends upon our response to it. Will our success result in a prideful sense of independence and boasting in our accomplishments? Or will we allow the success we enjoy to exalt the Lord? How much success can God entrust to us?

Run on to Success

It was a cold winter morning when Glenn Cunningham arrived at his schoolhouse on the Kansas prairie.[35] The teacher had not yet arrived, so Glenn and his brother Floyd decided to start a fire in the potbellied stove. After putting

---

[33] *Dallas Connection*, 75th Anniversary Issue.

[34] Quoted in "The Muscular Christianity of Eric Liddell," *Christianity Today* (June 14, 1985), p. 24

[35] For the complete story of his life, see Glenn Cunningham, *Never Quite* (Lincoln, VA: Chosen Books, 1981).

in the wood, they decided to pour on some kerosene to help it ignite.

Unknown to the boys, a community club, meeting in the school, had used the stove the night before and hot coals lay hidden under the gray ashes. And for some reason, gasoline had been left in the kerosene can. As the boys doused the wood, they were suddenly thrown against the wall of the schoolhouse by a fiery blast!

Floyd screamed, "I'm on fire!" Glenn realized that he was burning too. The two boys ran outside and threw themselves to the ground, rolling over and over to smother the flames. With their clothes half burned away, Floyd and Glenn began to run the two miles back to their home.

Father would expect us to make it, Glenn thought to himself. "Never quit, run on, work out your problems." That's what Clint Cunningham always told his boys. In spite of the agonizing pain, the boys managed to cover the two miles back to the farmhouse.

When the doctor arrived, he determined that there wasn't much that could be done for Floyd. His burns were deep and extensive. He died on the ninth morning after the accident. With Glenn, the problem was infection and scar tissue.

One afternoon as Glenn was recovering from his burns, he overheard a visitor tell his mother, "You may as well face it, my dear. Glenn is going to be an invalid the rest of his life." When his mother returned to the room, Glenn looked her in the eyes and declared, "I'm not going to be an invalid. I will walk, I will, I will!"

After six months Glenn was back on his feet, shuffling around with the help of a sturdy chair. In spite of the pain, he determined to recover the use of his red, scarred legs. Although he always encountered pain, he began walking to school again. Later he hopped, and eventually ran.

Glenn Cunningham went on to become the outstanding miler of his age and an Olympic medal winner. Between 1933 and 1940 he won twelve of thirty-one races in Madison Square Garden and set world records for the 800-meter race and the mile. In spite of his handicap, Glenn

Cunningham was impelled on to victory by his father's words, "Run on—never quit!"

God has revealed the key to success in life. We have discovered that key in Ecclesiastes 10:10, "Wisdom has the advantage of giving success." Yet we will never enjoy the prosperous and fulfilling future God has for us if we tuck this key away in a drawer. By applying God's key, we can run on to victory. And as we maintain an attitude of humility, giving God the glory, we can achieve spiritual objectives worth far more than an Olympic gold medal.

Now you have the key to success.

The decision to use it is up to *you*.

Made in the USA
San Bernardino, CA
08 May 2019